Dr. and

With sincere thanks —
and to whet their appetite
for more.

Alan G. Hughes

13 November 1975

Donated by

Professor John Ramsden

2008

D1614716

# A UNIQUE CONTRIBUTION TO INTERNATIONAL RELATIONS: THE STORY OF WILTON PARK

# A UNIQUE CONTRIBUTION
# TO INTERNATIONAL RELATIONS:
# THE STORY OF WILTON PARK

## DEXTER M. KEEZER

**London** · New York · St Louis · San Francisco · Düsseldorf
Johannesburg · Kuala Lumpur · Mexico · Montreal · New
Delhi · Panama · Paris · São Paulo · Singapore · Sydney
Toronto

Published by McGRAW–HILL Book Company (UK) Limited
Maidenhead · Berkshire · England

07 084424 0

PRINTED AND BOUND IN GREAT BRITAIN

# CONTENTS

# PREFACE AND ACKNOWLEDGEMENTS

After enjoying for the second time the privilege of participating, with my wife, in one of the international conferences held at Wilton Park in England I asked Henry Koeppler, its creator and leader, 'Where will I find a history of this most remarkable enterprise?'

'You won't', he replied, 'for none has been written. There are many bits and pieces but nothing that puts together the story as a whole'.

'Then', I said, 'I shall write a history of Wilton Park.'

This was a rather reckless thing to do. I am not a technically trained historian or biographer. I am an economist, with experience in journalism, business, and government who spent eight errant years as the president of an American college of liberal arts and sciences. This is not a technical background that certifies to my having what it takes to produce the sort of history Wilton Park deserves.

Even so, I suspect it was a good idea for me to undertake to write the history of Wilton Park. A controlling reason is that I am assured that no historian, with properly certified professional credentials, would ever dream of tackling the job. The documentation is much too sketchy for a history bearing professional hall marks—a deficiency emphasized early in my chronicle.

And yet it is very decidedly worth an effort to tell the fascinating and inspiring story of Wilton Park's first quarter century. In telling this story I make no pretense of having produced a full-blown history. My attention has been focused on:

1. The beginnings of Wilton Park when its student body was composed entirely of German prisoners of war;

2. How it evolved into a broadly international conference centre after a hairbreadth escape from extinction;

3. How it works and something of what it accomplishes internationally, and, perhaps pre-eminently,

4. The role of Henry Koeppler as the guiding genius of the enterprise.

Mine is what, I suppose, might be called an institutional analysis of Wilton Park. There remains an opportunity to do more than I have been able to do to place Wilton Park, in terms of action and reaction, in its larger British and international setting. If some brave and gifted historical synthetist can be tempted to do this, a great story of what almost miraculously has managed to be a great institution will be properly rounded out.

In what I have done I have had the co-operation of the present members of the Wilton Park academic staff, all

of whom are identified in my story. I also had the help of
K. Werner Lauermann, whose death while I was at work
on my chronicle deprived the academic staff of a towering
figure, to whom I pay tribute.

Sir Robert Birley, currently the Chairman of the Wilton
Park Academic Council, and a crucially important figure
in the development of Wilton Park, threw light for me
on its history which I would not have found otherwise.
So did Sir Frank Roberts who, as the United Kingdom's
Permanent Representative on the North Atlantic Council
from 1957–60 and as British Ambassador to the Federal
Republic of Germany from 1963 to 1968, was in key
positions to observe the impact in Europe of Wilton Park,
of which he is a staunch supporter. Sir Robert has been
good enough to write an illuminating foreword to my
story of Wilton Park. He has been too generous to me
personally, but this is the sort of excess of which I find
myself remarkably tolerant.

In dealing with the early history of Wilton Park I had
the help of talks with Alec Glasfurd and George H. D.
Greene who were members of the academic staff from its
beginnings in 1946 until they left together, by chance and
not by conspiracy, twelve years later. Mr Glasfurd went on
to a successful writing career and Mr Greene became head
of Merrion House, a school at Beaconsfield, the original
site of Wilton Park, which, in teaching advanced English
to students from overseas, embodies methods and ideas
which Mr Greene helped importantly to develop at Wilton
Park.

Erhard J. Dornberg, a participant in the first POW
sessions at Wilton Park who stayed on for some subsequent
sessions as its librarian, and who is now head of the Higher
Education Department of the State of North Rhine–
Westphalia, helped me by providing a sampling of those
who went on from Wilton Park to a broad range of leadership posts in the Federal Republic of Germany. I am

heavily indebted to him. I am similarly indebted to Mr and Mrs J. Noel Meinertzhagen, administrative officer and archivist at Wilton Park respectively, for helping me with much needed factual information.

I am also most grateful to the Rockefeller Foundation for having my wife and me as guests for a month at the Villa Serbelloni in Bellagio, Italy, where I found conditions ideal for doing intensive work on my study of Wilton Park. The good fortune of being at the Villa included having its Director, William C. Olson, a leader in American participation at Wilton Park and the first President of the American Friends of Wilton Park, available to give me help with my work, which he did abundantly. Professor William C. Rogers, Director of the World Affairs Center of the University of Minnesota, read a draft of my story of the Wilton Park enterprise and gave me some very helpful and feasible suggestions of ways to improve it. I thank him very much. For doing the same things I am also grateful to Clark W. Maser of San Francisco, California, the Chairman of the Board of Directors and a former President of the American Friends of Wilton Park.

I am indebted to The Johnson Foundation for hospitality extended to me and other participants in meetings in July 1972 at its home, Wingspread in Racine, Wisconsin, organized by the American Friends of Wilton Park. There, a promising start was made towards creating a Wilton Park in the United States, of which I take account in my chronicle.

My wife Anne knows more about the remote recesses in the basements of Wiston House with their dirt floors and accumulations of dust of the ages than she ever cared to know. For there she dug out and dug through oddly assorted old files seeking something that might throw light on the history and workings of Wilton Park. Her enthusiasm about Wilton Park is so great that she would regard any expression of gratitude as superfluous. But I make one anyway—for these and her many other labours in helping to put together a story of Wilton Park.

Dexter M. Keezer

# FOREWORD

I remember one day in 1947 standing in a garden in West Germany talking with a Dutch lady, who was one of several people of her country then spending what time they could in helping the German Evangelical Church. It was not surprising that nearly all of them had been in the Resistance Movement. She was explaining to me their motives. 'You see', she said, 'the last war was not the kind of war that was won by winning the war. Winning it had to come after it was over.' There was, I believe, a profound truth in this paradox. It lies at the heart of the decision to institute Wilton Park. It began as an attempt to help really to win the war. Simply defeating Germany on the field of battle was not enough. What was needed was for Germany, not only to repudiate Nazism, but herself to construct an alternative. It was to be done first by opening the eyes of young Germans, who were prisoners of war, to the world outside their own country, for Germany, during twelve years, had been to an extraordinary extent cut off from the rest of the world. And we in this country believed from our own experience that we could help best by enabling these young Germans to take part in free and open discussions, in which fear was wholly absent.

Perhaps some words of John Milton might be taken as the motto of Wilton Park. 'Where there is much desire to learn, there of necessity there will be much arguing, much writing, many opinions; for opinion in good men is but knowledge in the making.' There was no doubt about one thing, as anyone who attended sessions in the earliest days of Wilton Park will remember. There was certainly 'much desire to learn'.

There have been two turning points in the history of Wilton Park, which are both discussed in this book. The first was the decision to bring people over from Germany to take part in the sessions with the prisoners of war. I was in Germany at the time and I can remember the enthusiasm showed by those when they returned and how stimulating they had found their visits to be. The second was the decision of the Government in 1956 to close Wilton Park. Looking back on it now one can see that this was really something very fortunate. If Wilton Park had remained merely an Anglo–German institution it would have withered away before long. As the reader will find in this book, it was not destroyed, but it continued as an international institution. In this form it certainly has a continuing role to fulfil.

The reader of this book will find himself or herself coming to know a very unusual personality, Dr Heinz Koeppler, the Warden. I have known him now for many years and I have come to the conclusion that, besides the obvious qualities of efficiency and an ability to manage very different people, no less than four different characteristics were needed in the man who was to run Wilton Park if he was to make a success of it. First, he had to be a German. The very first need was to understand fully those who were members of the conferences. Second, he had to be an Englishman, for the contribution of Wilton Park was essentially an English one, derived from our national experience. Third, he had to have a quite unusual knowledge and understanding of international relations and of countries other than Germany and England. And, fourth, he had to have a really enthusiastic faith in the value of Wilton Park and all it stood for. The reader of this book will soon realize that the founder and Warden of Wilton Park most certainly had all these four characteristics. I might add that I suppose it is the fourth which makes him such a dangerous man in English public life. Many people have said to me that when invited by Heinz Koeppler to speak at Wilton Park there is no escape. You just know you have got to go.

This book is an account of a most remarkable experiment. It is written by someone not an Englishman or a German, and that is all to the good. It is written with enthusiasm, for Wilton Park generates enthusiasm. Yet the author has neither his feet off the ground nor his head in the clouds. He is well aware—one can see this, though he does not talk about it—that we are living in a difficult and dangerous age. Wilton Park is not a place where one just has an enjoyable fortnight. It is fighting a battle; it is engaged in trying to win a war. An Englishman who has been very much involved in Wilton Park from its earliest days can only feel grateful to the author for having written of this most unusual institution such a wise, spirited and readable an account.

Robert Birley

# 1

## AN EXPERIMENT
## WITHOUT A PRECEDENT

Can you imagine an enterprise devoted to increasing international enlightenment like this?

The sessions last only two weeks at most and some of them last only one week. Yet it so stirs the abiding loyalty and enthusiasm of many who have participated in these sessions that they form alumni associations, both in Europe and North America, to help advance its work.

About 85 per cent of the money to pay its bills comes from the national government of the country where it is located. Yet this government scrupulously sees to it that it has complete academic freedom.

To lead discussions with at most a few score of participants in its sessions it manages to recruit, among others of comparable distinction, the highest political leaders in its land. In the discussions, these men and women submit themselves to searching questions about the policies they are following and trenchant comments on these policies by people from other lands.

There is, in fact, an enterprise which has these among other remarkable characteristics. It is Wilton Park, in England, an enterprise dedicated to 'The formation of an informed international public opinion'.

Wilton Park recently celebrated its twenty-fifth anniversary with a Jubilee Conference. The British Prime Minister, Edward Heath, had an engagement to open the discussion at this conference. He also had on his hands the problem of dealing for his party with a grave labour and political tangle in Scotland. What to do? The Prime Minister left the tangle and dramatically dropped in by helicopter to keep his engagement with Wilton Park.[1] And for the balance of the Jubilee Conference he was followed by a galaxy of leaders in international and British public affairs as discussion leaders, as he had been preceded in the same daring capacity by Harold Wilson, his predecessor as Prime Minister of Great Britain, when Mr Wilson was leader of the parliamentary Opposition. Those who, in addition to the Prime Minister, led discussions at the Jubilee Conference are listed in Appendix A, which presents the conference programme.

The principal creator of Wilton Park and the presiding genius over the quarter century it has been at work is Heinz or Henry Koeppler. Both the German and English

---

1. Perhaps there were security forces hidden in the shrubbery around the croquet lawn where the Prime Minister's helicopter landed. But the only visible protection was provided by a small truck, poised to spring into action if the helicopter caught on fire in landing and a member of the truck's crew dressed in a silver coloured fireproof suit. The lack of visible security forces somehow strengthened the feeling that the security problem was well in hand.

versions of his given name are used, fittingly enough in the light of his career. Here the English version, Henry, will be used. He has the title of Warden, a distinguished title that does not have the penal connotation it does in the United States. It is roughly synonymous with the German title *Rektor* or the French *Monsieur le Recteur*. His title in the very early days of Wilton Park was Principal but it was soon changed to Warden, selected from a considerable variety of titles used to designate the head of an Oxford College.

This effort to tell the story of Wilton Park, as it has unfolded over the past twenty-five years, is a testimonial to the esteem in which the institution is held by one of its American alumni. The success of the effort will best be gauged by the extent to which it prompts others who have been at Wilton Park to add improvements to the chronicle. There is vast room for improvement. The archives of Wilton Park, suffering from chronic financial under-nourishment and perhaps also from being less than a major concern of a staff strongly inclined to look towards tomorrow rather than at yesterday, are often sketchy and sometimes less than that. Most of the best parts of the story of Wilton Park are in the minds and hearts of those— now well over 12 000 men and women widely scattered over several continents—who have been there.

To get to Wilton Park, you go to the beautiful medieval market town of Steyning, a few miles north of the English Channel and not far from Brighton. A reminder of Steyning's venerability is to be found in the fact that Aethelwulf, father of the greatest of the Saxon Kings, Alfred (849–899?), was buried in the yard of the Norman church, now used by the town parish, until his remains were moved to Winchester Cathedral.

The shortest route to Wilton Park from Steyning is along Mouse Lane. As befits a mouse lane, it is very narrow and a veritable tunnel part of the way, completely arched over by trees and worn almost to ravine depth by travel and erosion during the centuries. In about a mile Mouse Lane leads into a beautiful rolling park which has as a backdrop a section of England's South Downs, crowned by the Chanctonbury Ring of great beech trees.[1] It is country which Rudyard Kipling, who had a home base not far away for his travels over much of the world, thought some of the most beautiful he had ever seen.

Standing serenely on a rise in the park is Wiston House, a massive, mostly Elizabethan manor house with its even older church close by. This is the present seat of Wilton Park.

To have Wilton Park at Wiston House in Wiston Park is confusing and calls for explanation. This is found in the fact that Wilton Park began operations, in January 1946, in a park of that name surrounding a manor house in Beaconsfield, Buckinghamshire. When, late in 1950, its operations were moved south to Wiston House the name Wilton Park had come to mean so much to so many people that it was taken along. So now it is Wilton Park at Wiston House.

The initial impetus for what was to become Wilton Park came from Winston Churchill, then wartime Prime Minister of Great Britain. Towards what finally promised to be the victorious end of the Second World War in Europe, he circulated an intra-governmental memorandum, now lost in or from the files, which one of those who read it remembers as beginning, in authentic Churchillian style, 'Every ounce of energy must be put to the successful prosecution of the war, but now that the sun of victory is rising over the horizon, . . would appropriate Departments turn their minds to the post-war period? . . .'

Henry Koeppler, then Assistant Director of the German Region of the Political Warfare Executive, which was also

1. This ring of trees provides some of the scenic background for John Galsworthy's *Forsyte Saga*.

known as the Political Intelligence Department of the British Foreign Office, had been thinking a lot about the post-war period. He had been thinking particularly about measures that, after the military defeat of Germany, would help that nation to have a tolerably good chance of leaving behind its devastating Nazi period and again becoming a good and co-operative neighbour in the relatively demo-cratic western European world.

Henry Koeppler's background made such a range of concern come naturally. He had been born on 30 June 1912, and spent his early boyhood in Wollstein, a town about 100 miles east of Berlin which at the time was in the heart of Prussia. When, in 1919, the post-First World War Treaty of Versailles again placed Wollstein within the borders of Poland, as it had been before the second division of the country in 1793, Henry's father, a loyal German who enjoyed wealth and prosperity in Wollstein as an expert in potato farming, left and took his family to Berlin.

There Henry Koeppler grew up. For a year (1930–31) he was a student at the University of Berlin. Then, after a term at Heidelberg, he studied at the University of Kiel in Schleswig-Holstein until mid-year 1933. At the University of Kiel he demonstrated a capacity for political leadership among the students by being elected Student President of Christian Albert House. This establishment was initially called Bergmann House, the name of its wealthy Swedish founder, who felt that students who gave clear promise of becoming German university professors should know something of their contemporaries from other countries. Bergmann House provided spartan accommodation for about 40 students working in a broad range of academic disciplines, one third of whom came from abroad and all of whom were hopefully certified as prospective profes-sorial material. When the money provided by the founder ran out, the House was taken over by the University of

Kiel and re-christened Christian Albert House, in honour of the Danish prince who founded the university.

Both in the international composition of its residents and in the wide range of academic studies brought together there, Christian Albert House had an important influence in shaping ideas which Henry Koeppler would develop at Wilton Park.

### From Germany to Oxford to war

At Christian Albert House Henry Koeppler also developed an academic competence which he demonstrated by going to Oxford, England, in October, 1932 and winning a competition for a scholarship which enabled him to carry on his studies at Oxford University the following year. This he did with great distinction for the three years 1933–36 and earned his D Phil Degree.

In 1937, at the youthful age of 25, he was appointed Lecturer by the Board of the Faculty of Modern History of Oxford University and Senior Demy of Magdalen College. Both of these titles are rather opaque for those who are not Oxonians and the meaning of the title Demy is a mystery to some who are. There seems to be agreement that it is derived from the French demi or half, and is the title of a teacher or 'a foundation scholar at Magdalen College', as the Oxford Dictionary defines it, who performs the duties of a tutor but receives only a fraction of the pay of a fully accredited tutor. Remarkably enough, at Oxford, Modern History is treated as covering all history since the Greek and Roman and thus accounts for the fact that Henry Koeppler was appointed as a Lecturer in Modern History even though his field of concentration was Medieval European History.

He held his posts as University Lecturer and Magdalen College Demy until war came in 1939. His reputation as a scholar in the field of Medieval European History had been established by his study of the pragmatic origins of

Modern European universities, the results of which were presented in an article entitled 'Frederick Barbarossa and the Schools of Bologna', published in the *English Historical Review* for October 1939.[1]

As current international issues became more and more compelling and strident during the latter part of the 'thirties, on the way to the Second World War, Henry Koeppler found himself paying more attention to them and less to medieval history. In following this course he was strongly influenced by talks he had at Oxford with Gilbert Murray. 'Talks with him before the last war', Warden Koeppler subsequently wrote, 'served to sow the seed from which Wilton Park grew'.[2] Professor Murray gladly gave up building a greater and greater monument for himself as a classical scholar to respond to demands upon him as a teacher, interpreter of current events and worker against militarism and for international peace. Like Henry Koeppler he had come to England as an immigrant (from Australia) and in 1886, as an undergraduate at St John's College, Oxford, 'He had already foreshadowed his international activities in a motion at the Oxford Union (the Students' Parliament) calling the free nations to unite against German and Russian militarism'. In his house 'the duty to respond to present demands was paramount, and he was too busy to take much thought for posterity's opinion of his work'.[3]

Inspired to make much the same sort of response to the international events swirling about him, Henry Koeppler collaborated in writing a book entitled *A Lasting Peace*[4] which was addressed to the desperate difficulty of securing

1. The *English Historical Review*, No. CCXVI, October 1939, p. 577.
2. *Wilton Park Journal*, No. 34, January 1966, p. 4.
3. Entry about George Gilbert Aimé Murray by M. I. Henderson in the *Dictionary of National Biography* (1951–60), Oxford University Press, 1971, pp. 757–761.
4. *A Lasting Peace* by Maxwell Garnett and H. F. Koeppler, George Allen and Unwin, London, 1940.

one. The opening sentence in the Koeppler section of the book is 'There can be no Anglo–German understanding without France', an affirmation of his conviction that there could be no lasting peace without broad and at the time seemingly quite improbable co-operation.

Henry Koeppler also spent much of his time contrasting the political ways of Britain and of Nazi Germany under Hitler, an enterprise for which he was singularly equipped by his background. In fact he developed this theme so vigorously that George Gordon, the President of Magdalen College at the time, said to him, in 1937, 'You are always talking about this fellow Hitler. Why don't you teach a course about him and his significance?' So he did.

His knowledge of Nazi Germany and its complete incompatibility with his political ideals prompted him to accept gratefully the help of his Oxford College in becoming a British citizen in 1937 and, with the coming of the Second World War in 1939, to go to work with a section of a British Government Department concentrating on the military defeat of Nazi Germany through political warfare, where he ultimately became Assistant Director of the German Region.

His experience in Germany, at Oxford and in the German Region of the Political Warfare Executive also led him to respond to Winston Churchill's request for thinking about the post-war period with the proposal of a programme to meet some of the post-war political needs in Germany, of which his experience made him poignantly aware.

Like the Churchill memorandum which prompted it, a copy of the Koeppler proposal cannot be found in the files, perhaps because, by a standard process of bureaucratic osmosis, its substance had been absorbed by higher authority in the Department. But the distinctive part of its design is visible. It was to bring Germans likely to have consequential roles in shaping post-war public opinion (and hence the character of their country) to

England, and there to encourage them to discuss problems, primarily political problems of mutual interest and importance, as mature, independent thinking individuals, something that had been sternly and, if necessary, violently discouraged during the years of Nazi domination.

J. Martin Lindsay, a staff member at Wilton Park (in the years 1947–50) subsequently phrased the central problem to which Henry Koeppler's proposal was addressed in this way: 'Hitler had very little use for the German people. As the end approached, he informed Speer (Albert Speer, Hitler's Minister of Armaments) that he intended that a people that had shown itself so unworthy of him should be destroyed; and from the beginning he had not the slightest intention that the German people would be trusted to think for themselves. We are now having to deal with this long night of mental isolation'.[1]

## A residential college at POW Camp 300

The general structure Henry Koeppler had in mind was that of the English residential college which he, as one who had had much of his education in Germany, had found so intellectually invigorating and so conducive to respect for freedom and the democratic political process. Even a few weeks in such an environment would, he was convinced, give much encouragement to Germans sharing in it to go in the right direction in helping to form post-war public opinion at home—a direction which for him was that of political freedom, democracy and intellectual integrity. It would accomplish more in providing such impetus, he was sure, than the regimented administration of a rigid anti-Nazi programme of German 're-education'. 'Re-education', he said, 'is a horse born of ignorance, out of arrogance, and with such a pedigree will never win a race'.[2]

1. Memorandum, to Dr Koeppler, 14 February 1948.
2. *Notes on Wilton Park*, February 1949, p. 2.

Strictly as an experiment, with 'experiment' heavily underlined, Henry Koeppler was given the opportunity to lead in the sort of programme he had proposed by being made its academic director or principal, which was initially his title. But it was with a dramatically different sort of student body and in a vastly different setting than that which he had had initially in mind. The first student body in Wilton Park, also known as POW Camp 300, was composed entirely of German prisoners of war. And so were successive student bodies—of about 300 for each session lasting from six to eight weeks—during the first year of its operation, 1946–47.

From German prisoners of war held in England and North Africa—about 400 000 of them—these POWs had volunteered and been chosen for an intensive course at Wilton Park with its major objectives

(1) to make them more effective leaders in the study and discussion programmes being conducted on a large scale in the prison camps from which they came, and

(2) to increase their capacity, when they were re-patriated to help lead public opinion in post-war Germany in the direction of responsible individualism and democracy.

Few unregenerate Nazis or other political extremists were enrolled at Wilton Park, at least knowingly. In the case of the few avowed Nazis who were enrolled, the purpose was to give them the eye-popping experience of seeing a free wheeling democratic operation at work.

Some of the methods used at other POW camps to determine the political convictions of volunteers for Wilton Park, and whether or not they should be accepted, were subtle. One of those in the first group of POWs, then 20 years old, recalls some of the questions he was asked.

One was, 'Is Karl Marx alive and living in Moscow?'
He confessed that he didn't know for sure whether Karl
Marx was alive or dead or where he might be—a confession
that suggested that he would not qualify as much of a
Communist. His interrogator also read him part of a
poem by Heinrich Heine, the German poet who was a
Jew, and asked him if he knew the poem. He replied that
he not only knew it but could recite the balance of the
poem if asked to do so—a respose that strongly indicated
that he was not much of a Nazi. So he stayed at Wilton
Park and is now one of the educational leaders of Western
Germany.

Of his student body when Wilton Park was POW Camp
300, Henry Koeppler has recalled that he worked 'with
German soldiers of all ranks from privates to generals,
with convinced anti-Nazis who had paid for their convictions by being put into penal battalions, with people who
thought that the only thing wrong with Hitler was that
he had lost, and above all with young men whose whole
world, the only one they had ever known, had been shattered
and who felt lost and bewildered'.[1]

The student-prisoners lived together in those standard
units of emergency housing, Nissen huts—an arrangement
which initially horrified some of the higher ranking officers.
The huts were clustered around the manor house at Wilton
Park, Beaconsfield, which doubled as faculty quarters
and as a post of command. There was still barbed wire
around the camp, although it was apparently not manned
by guards so as to be closely confining. Kingsley Martin,
who gave a lecture at one of the earliest sessions, found
that 'any prisoner could escape if he wished, but none do,
or wish to do so'.[2]

1. 'Purpose, Aims and Methods of Wilton Park', the opening statement
   at the 25th Anniversary Jubilee Conference, *Wilton Park Journal*
   No. 46, March, 1972, p. 15.
2. The *New Statesman and Nation*, 6 April 1946, p. 252.

Within the barbed wire, however, the creature comforts were no greater than those at any of the other prison camps and the working day was long—generally from 8.30 a.m. to 10.00 p.m.

What was decidedly different, however, was the intellectual freedom inside the barbed wire. Those chosen for Wilton Park were given the opportunity for study and discussion of thorny problems in an atmosphere of honest give and take, designed to make them influential in spreading faith in such procedures when they returned to the prison camps from which they had been chosen, as virtually all of them did, or later when they went on to repatriation in Germany. Only a few of the POWs at Wilton Park were directly repatriated. These included some special hardship cases and some who were at Wilton Park for several sessions as staff assistants.

In a speech opening the first session of Wilton Park on 17 January 1946,[1] Major General Sir Kenneth Strong, the Director-General of the Political Intelligence Department of the British Foreign Office, characterized it as 'an experiment that has no precedent in previous war and post-war periods'.[2]

Outlining what it was hoped to accomplish he said, 'We believe that an attempt must be made to bridge the gap in trends of thought between victor and vanquished'—

1. 'Address at Wilton Park Training Centre', printed as an appendix to *Intelligence at the Top—The Recollections of an Intelligence Officer* by Major General Sir Kenneth Strong, KBE, CB.; A Giniger book, published in association with Cassell-London, 1968.
2. It could be argued that there was at least a partial precedent for what was being undertaken for and with German POWs at Wilton Park. In the fall of 1944, over a year before the opening of Wilton Park, the United States Army had launched what ultimately became a large scale programme designed to give democracy in post-war Germany a better chance by giving German POWs selected from about 370 000 of them in the United States courses in the ways, means, and constructive significance of democracy. About 25 000 POWs in the United States were enrolled in these courses which, as stated by one of their leaders Henry W. Ehrmann, had as their major function 'to assist in the development of a democratic leadership'. He described the aims and methods

a statement which might have provided some of the inspiration for the decision to call the camp newspaper *Die Bruecke*—the bridge—after the first few issues, when it was called *Der Anruf*—the call.

## Making partners of prisoners

In outlining the curriculum, as it had been worked out by the academic staff, General Strong stressed the element of teamwork in making it effective. 'A large part of the course', he said, 'will be devoted to working out with you [the POWs] the main points of German development during the past eighty or hundred years. I say purposely "with you", for your active co-operation in everything that happens here is an indispensible condition for the success of the experiment'.

'You will not only listen to lectures but' he promised, 'you will have the opportunity of taking part in subsequent discussion'—certainly a boldly experimental promise to a group composed entirely of prisoners of war. Asked subsequently why an historical study of eighty to one hundred years of the German route to the disaster of the Second World War was required, Henry Koeppler remarked that 'the theory is that the maggot got into the apple long before Hitler'.[1]

As part of the Wilton Park curriculum the British political and social scene would be explored and explained, and in some measure directly observed, not as a model for

1. *The* (London) *Weekly News*, 15 March 1947.

of the schools and the criteria used in selecting candidates 'their suitability for public functions in Allied-occupied Germany' in an article 'An Experiment in Political Education: The Prisoner-of-War Schools in the United States', in *Social Research*, **14**, pp. 304–320, September 1947. A more vivid and comprehensive popular account was published by Quentin Reynolds under the title, 'Experiment in Democracy', in *Colliers* magazine of 25 May 1946.

However, there were enough differences in the auspices, general design and methods of Wilton Park, as compared with the United States Army programme with the same general objectives, to justify General Strong's characterization of Wilton Park as an experiment without precedent.

post-war Germany or any other place but as a contribution to German understanding, perhaps inspiring, of how one relatively democratic set of institutions worked relatively well. This would necessarily lead to some concentration on the relation between the individual and the state and the pathology of this relationship under the Nazi regime. International relations, particularly in terms of the organizations burgeoning right after the end of the Second World War in the hope of dealing with them constructively, would be studied both for potential pitfalls and opportunities for making the world a more civilized place.

In his welcoming speech General Strong reiterated his emphasis on co-operation and teamwork, in the British academic style, as the key to the success of Wilton Park. He said, 'We have set up this Training Centre on the model of the British Residential Colleges, establishments where people pursuing collective intellectual studies live and work together. The art of creating a free community is that of living and working in harmony . . .'

The fifteen tutors were all British citizens. Some, still in the army, draped academic robes over their uniforms when teaching. The title of tutor had been transplanted from Oxford where it was and remains a badge of intellectual distinction. Later, when Wilton Park was to become broadly international, the title of tutor, which means a variety of different things in different countries, including the purveyor of emergency aid for the academic laggard, was dropped and the perhaps more generally understandable but quite non-committal title of 'member of the academic staff' was substituted.[1] At Wilton Park at Beaconsfield each tutor worked with a group of 25 to 30 POWs in covering the ground, much of it very sensitive political terrain, prescribed by the curriculum.

1. The British Foreign Office still uses the title of tutor, which basically
means simply one who provides tuition, in making appointments of
hose who at Wilton Park are called members of the academic staff.

**Always a full house for VIPs**

To spare his VIP lecturers the possible unhappiness of talking to a handfull of POWs in a Nissen hut (or Quonset in American terminology) with 300 yawning seats, Henry Koeppler developed an ingenious arrangement. It reflected his abiding conviction that the overall size of the audience is generally less important to most speakers than having the audience sufficient to fill the available seats—a conviction which, acted upon, probably has more than a little to do with his phenomenal success in persuading leading public figures in Britain and Western Europe to open discussions at Wilton Park. He installed curtains of sail cloth, the only material available at the time, which could be lowered at different distances from the front of the Nissen hut lecture hall. If only a small group showed up for a lecture a curtain was lowered, before the arrival of the speaker, to block off all but the few seats needed so that there would be a capacity crowd. At some lectures there would be a rustling behind the curtain signalling the late arrival of another contingent of listeners, so the curtain would be raised to enlarge the visible audience. On occasion several curtains would be raised in succession as the crowd swelled—to the surprise but not, the Principal was convinced, to the disappointment of the speaker.[1]

At the evening lectures care was taken to have a broad range of subject matter presented by a wide variety of authorities—writers, academicians, broadcasters, labour leaders, politicians. Lady Astor, Rose Macaulay, Lord Beveridge, Lord Lindsay of Birker, Gilbert Murray, Harold Nicholson and Arnold J. Toynbee were among those who talked to the POWs at their evening sessions. One of the tutors of the time recalls the incredulity that

---

1. It has been suggested that this was an application of what should be celebrated as Koeppler's law for satisfying speakers. The law might run 'A full house is far more important in satisfying a speaker than the size of the crowd'.

c

Bertrand Russell created on the part of one of his German listeners by his evening lecture on 'The Philosophy of Power' at one of the early Wilton Park sessions. 'Do you think that was *the* Bertrand Russell?' the incredulous member of his audience was overheard to say as he left the lecture hut. 'I cannot believe it. A world famous philosopher and I could understand every word he said.' But it really was Bertrand Russell.

When the evening lectures were by politicians, care was taken to have a balanced representation of the major British political faiths. Conservative, Labour and Liberal Members of Parliament all had their innings and in the process reinforced the idea that Wilton Park was not purveying a standard line of political doctrine. A. L. Lloyd, a visitor to Wilton Park in its very early days, reported that 'What Tory Lord Soulbury says one evening may be contradicted by Labourite R. H. Crossman the next . . . a Brains Trust of Labour MPs may follow one of Conservative MPs'. Mr Lloyd quoted the Principal as saying of this procedure, 'The pupils get different answers to their questions, but that's good for them; it's something non-totalitarian; they learn there is no single official answer'.[1]

After giving an evening lecture at Wilton Park, W. W. Astor, MP, wrote, 'As several previous lecturers had been supporters of Mr Atlee (Prime Minister and leader of the dominant Labour Party) I was encouraged to state the Conservative case vigorously. So Tory history and principles were discussed and the merits of Nationalization *v.* Private Enterprise debated. . . . The Conservative contention that Government monopolies tended to be inefficient was challenged. I pointed out that every plane designed by the Air Ministry before the war had proved a flop, while the planes that defeated the Luftwaffe . . . all

---

1. 'Can German Prisoners Learn Democracy?' by A. L. Lloyd, *Picture Post*, London, 6 April 1946, p. 13.

owed their existence to private aircraft firms going against
the Air Ministry's views. I then suggested that if our
aircraft industry had been nationalized before the war
I would probably now be in the audience and they would
be lecturing me, a point they took uproariously'.[1]

Of the give and take at the evening lectures Harold
Nicholson, the eminent writer and authority on diplomacy
in its political setting who subsequently became one of
Wilton Park's key advisors, wrote:

> I lectured for some forty minutes, and thereafter
> there were questions which lasted for almost an hour
> and a half. It must be realized that the Commandant
> of the prison camp was present, as well as the Principal
> and the tutors of the training course; yet, there was no
> sign whatsoever that the prisoners were deterred from
> asking leading questions by the presence of their gaolers.
> In fact, one man asked me why it was, if we disapproved
> of Prussian discipline and Nazi methods, that we our-
> selves adopted such methods in our prison camps.
> I knew that he was referring, not to the British officers
> in charge of the camp, but to the German NCOs who
> in the earlier stages of the war were perhaps given too
> much authority. I ignored this distinction and asked
> him in my turn whether he would have dared to put
> such a question to a visitor in the presence of the
> Commandant of Dachau or Buchenwald. The prisoners
> laughed heartily at this comparison.[2]

Perhaps the laughter was partly prompted by the fact that
Mr Nicolson had artfully ducked the question.

1. 'Teaching Them Free Speech', by the Hon. W. W. Astor, *Daily Graphic*,
   31 December 1946.
2. Marginal comment in *The Spectator*, 1 March 1946, p. 218.

**Accommodations for conflicting political faiths**

There was also a balanced representation of conflicting British political faiths in the staff of tutors. Two of them who came to Wilton Park in its very early days and carried on together as anchor men through its first quarter century typify the spread of political convictions in the tutorial staff. Robert D. J. Gibson, a Cambridge University graduate, who signed on as a tutor in May 1946 and who is now Dean and Chief Administrator of Wilton Park at Wiston House, is a staunch Conservative in politics. During the war he had spent five years as a civilian prisoner of the Germans in Holland, Germany and Austria after being captured in 1940 while trying to get members of his family back to England from Holland. K. Werner Lauermann, a Czechoslovak citizen and a refugee from Nazi Germany who first came to Wilton Park as a lecturer in February 1946 and two years later joined the tutorial staff as a full time member which, with one brief interruption, he remained until his tragically premature death in October 1971, was well on the other side of the political spectrum to the left. He thought it was moderately accurate to characterize him as a Democratic Socialist. During their close association for almost twenty-five years, Mr Gibson and Mr Lauermann remained impressed by the other's political obtuseness, but they also remained close personal and professional friends.

A printer by trade, Mr Lauermann helped the Press Class with its printing. When the move was made to Wiston House he preserved a physical link with Wilton Park at Beaconsfield by bringing the hand typesetting equipment used there along with him. In a print shop established in the basement of Wiston House, which pre-dates Gutenberg by some centuries, and with type and type-setting methods that don't seem very much post-Gutenberg, Mr Lauermann continued, until his death, to set the Wilton Park conference programmes by hand, except for

an interlude of a year in 1953 which he spent at the Asian
Trade Union College in Calcutta, India, as Advisor to the
Director of Trade Union Education in Asia.

### Civilians join the POWs

At the end of the first year, in January 1947, there was a
change in the composition of the student body which was
to have a decisive effect on the future of Wilton Park.
At the suggestion of General Sir Brian Robertson, Chief
of the British zone of military occupation in Germany,
German civilians were sent from the different zones of
Allied occupation, first from the British zone and later
from the American and French zones, to join the POWs
at Wilton Park.

General Robertson's idea was that this was one way to
broaden the outlook of people who would be needed in
leadership posts in Germany. For the next year and a
half, until mid-1948, an average of about fifty German
civilians, both men and women, representing a broad
spectrum of occupations and professions, joined about
250 German prisoners of war to make up the student
body of about 300 for each six-week session.

Understandably enough, the combining of civilians and
prisoners of war got off to a rather bumpy start. Among
the reasons, as related by one who was there at the time,
were that POWs resented the fact that the civilians could
be at home in Germany if they elected to be, while the
prisoners had no such choice. And the civilians tended to be
resentful of the fact that the POWs had a much higher
standard of living than civilians were having in Germany.
Before long, however, relations between the two groups
became comfortable enough, and the coming of the civilians
had the major effect of making it possible to continue
Wilton Park when all of the prisoners of war left England
in mid-June 1948. It provided a bridge, or *Die Bruecke*,
for continuing Wilton Park as an all-civilian enterprise—

a course strongly urged by Robert Birley who at the time was Educational Advisor to the Military Governor of the British Control Commission in Germany and who subsequently became one of the key figures in the development of Wilton Park. The decision was made to continue the experiment on this basis, again with the primary purpose of helping Germans likely to have positions of leadership in their country to broaden their perspective on Anglo-German and international affairs, and to increase their capacity to participate constructively in a democratic Germany and Europe.

About forty-five hundred German prisoners of war had been at Wilton Park sessions between January 1946 and June 1948. Anything like a total assessment of what had been accomplished by this unique enterprise is obviously impossible. But there are some significant fragments of contemporary appraisal.

In the last of fifteen issues of the Camp magazine, Jennie Lee, (Mrs Aneurin Bevan), a Member of Parliament, wrote, 'In all the bitterness and fear left by the war, Wilton Park will always remain for me a happy memory in a barbarous world. By doing a civilized job with delicacy and intelligence, it will, I am sure, recall the better side of English life to many who came here as prisoners and, I hope, have left as friends'.[1]

Mr R. H. S. Crossman, also a Member of Parliament and subsequently a Senior Cabinet Minister reported in the same farewell issue of the camp magazine, ' . . . it has been a frequently repeated pleasure to discover, on my visits to Germany, that someone who is really putting his or her back into the job of reconstruction turns out to be an Old Wiltonian'.[1]

Mr Peter Calvocoressi, Secretary of the Liberal Party Foreign Affairs Committee, wrote, 'Wilton Park . . . has

1. *Wilton Park*, Special Edition, Fifteenth Course, May–June 1948, p. 1.

made the most important contribution, namely the first contribution, to the restoration of a free Anglo–German exchange of ideas and information, without which mutual understanding and good will and therefore also the preservation of peace are impossible'.[1]

One quite immediate reflection of the esteem in which its prisoner-of-war students held Wilton Park was the organization of groups of 'Old Wiltonians' in the prison camps from which they had come. Patrick Gordon Walker, a Member of Parliament who also later became a Cabinet Minister, wrote of this development in this way:

> Each student gets a copy of *Die Bruecke* at the end of the course—treasured by many as a sort of old school tie.... The old school tie aspect of Wilton Park has caused some problems. Dr Koeppler, Principal of the School, was an undergraduate at Oxford, to which he came after his education in Germany. He himself has experienced the impact of British education on a German. So successful has he been in awakening the loyalty of his students to the continuing standards and traditions of this most recent of boarding schools that some resentment has been caused by the return of the Old Wilton Park Boys to their camps around the country. Those prisoners know they have been to the best school in the prisoner-of-war world. Wilton Park Clubs have also spontaneously sprung up in Germany. The authorities have sought to check these developments by banning the use of the name Wilton Park. It would be easier to break the public school tradition by rechristening Eton 'Windsor Multilateral School'.[2]

The enthusiasm of the POWs was no passing fancy. This was convincingly demonstrated at a weekend meeting

1. Ibid. p. 3.
2. '*Weekend at Wilton Park*', by Patrick Gordon Walker, MP, in *The Changing Nation*. Contact Book, January 1948.

of a large number of 'Old Wiltonians' in Hennef, West Germany, in July 1953. Henry Koeppler, who led discussions at the meeting, reported that 'about 20 per cent of those who came had been to Wilton Park as prisoners-of war'. On his trip to Germany, he also found Old Wiltonian clubs in Hanover, Berlin, Munich, Nuremberg, Stuttgart and Cologne that 'had been active for a considerable number of years'.[1]

**A take-off for many notable careers**
In the years ahead there would be many more manifestations of the influence of Wilton Park on the POWs who were there, as they gained eminence in Germany as did many in politics, education, the professions, and industry. And the same thing would be true of the civilians who came from Germany to join the prisoners of war from January 1947 until mid-year 1948 when all the prisoners were repatriated.

At the Jubilee Conference, celebrating the twenty-fifth anniversary of Wilton Park, there were four participants, all of whom had been at its early POW sessions. One was P. Paul Jost, an eminent architect and a member of the Parliament of the Palatinate; the second was Erhard J. Dornberg, Head of the Higher Education Department in the Ministry of Education of the State of North Rhine–Westphalia; the third was Hans-Dieter Schulz, a leading journalist and the television commentator of Berlin; and the fourth was C. Zodel, Editor-in-Chief of *Schwabische Zeitung* of Leutkirch/Allgau. Of Mr Jost his companion Erhard Dornberg subsequently wrote, 'the real value and contribution of Wilton Park is to have helped people like Paul Jost. . . . Without Wilton Park Herr Jost might have become a good architect only. His "outstanding achievement" is to have helped make democracy work in Trier and the Palatinate for over 20 years, as Chairman

1. Memorandum to MOW, 20 July 1953.

of the Social Democrats, the minority party, in Trier, criticizing and co-operating, and now as a member of the Palatinate Parliament. He would have made more money without giving some of his time to politics, but Trier, his home town, has now better social services, hospitals, schools and so on. And there are many others like him', of whom Mr Dornberg listed a score.

Here, listed alphabetically, are some of those who went on from very early Wilton Park sessions to eminence in political life in the Federal German Republic in all of its major political parties: Rainer Barzel, Chairman of the Christian Democratic party and leader of the Opposition in the Bundestag; Karl-Wilhelm Berkhan, Parliamentary Secretary of State in the Federal Ministry of Defence; Ralf Dahrendorf, Parliamentary Secretary of State in the Foreign Office of the German Federal Republic and German Commissioner in the European Economic Community in Brussels; Horst Grabert, Senator of Berlin; Johann Baptist Gradl, former Minister of the Federal German Republic; Hildegard Hamm-Brücher, Parliamentary Secretary of State in the Federal Ministry of Science and Learning; Winfried Hedergott, former Vice-President and Chairman of the Free Democratic party in the Parliament of Lower Saxony; Karl Hemfler, Minister of Justice in the State of Hesse; Hermann Hoecherl, former Federal Minister of Agriculture; Alois Hundhammer, former Minister of State of Bavaria; Wilhelm Kaisen, former Head of the Land Government and Lord Mayor of the State of Bremen; Heinrich Köppler, leader of the Christian Democratic party Opposition in the State of North Rhine–Westphalia, former Secretary of State; Lauritz Lauritzen, Minister of Housing of the Federal Republic; and Willi Weyer, Home Secretary of the State of North Rhine–Westphalia.

Indicative of the esteem in which Wilton Park is held by some of its most illustrious German alumni is this little bit of history. On a week's visit to England, at the invitation of the British government, Rainer Barzel was asked what he would like to do on the one day in the week that was not programmed for him. He said that he would like to go back to Wilton Park which had meant so much to him. On a similar visit as a guest of the British government Gerhard Mueller, President of the German Constitutional Court, the highest court in Germany, was asked the same question about how he would like to spend his free day and he made the same choice—to go back to Wilton Park for a visit.

The route to political eminence for some who had been at Wilton Park was made much rougher because they had been there. Dr Willy Brundert, who ultimately became Lord Mayor of Frankfurt, was one of these. After attending the first POW session at Wilton Park in 1946, he returned to his home in Saxe/Anhalt in East Germany where he became Deputy Minister of Economics. Working on the distribution of power resources between East and West Germany, he was charged with favouring West Germany, was arrested and made the defendant in a 'show trial' in 1950. Among the charges pressed against him was that he had been trained at that 'notorious training school for imperialists, saboteurs and agents, Wilton Park'. He managed to get to the West where he ultimately gained political renown as the Lord Mayor of the city of Frankfurt.

There was sometimes suspicion much nearer home about what Wilton Park was up to. A year or so after it had moved to its present quarters Henry Koeppler was quoted as saying, 'Half the village thought we were training spies to work in Germany. The other half thought we were training German spies to work in Britain. Now, I think most of them realize that our work is of some importance'.[1]

At the same time there were some complaints both about what it was understood Wilton Park was doing and the

1. *The Sunday Chronicle*, 10 February 1952.

cost to the British taxpayer of doing it. Early in 1952
under the editorial heading 'Cozy for the Germans',
*The Financial Times* complained that 'The elegant gentlemen of the Foreign Office still maintain a costly seminary
in this country for the improvement of the German mind',
and testily inquired, 'Why should the British taxpayer
bear the burden of providing select groups of Germans
with cozy, intellectual holidays in the Sussex country-
side?'

**Esteem, respect, and ultimately affection**

But on the whole a remarkably large element of good will,
both internally and externally, seems to have permeated
the operations of Wilton Park from the outset. One
remarkable aspect of this was the success which Henry
Koeppler had, as Principal and then as Warden, in gaining
the esteem and respect of so many Germans who participated in the Wilton Park enterprise right from its POW
beginnings. He had renounced his German citizenship
and become a British subject after Hitler came to power.
He had been engaged on the British side in political warfare
against Germany. And his first Wilton Park student
bodies at POW Camp 300 were prisoners because of the
Allied victory to which he had contributed. Why then was
Henry Koeppler's effectiveness as a leader of these Wilton
Park POW student bodies not corroded by resentment
that he had changed allegiances?

There probably was some corrosion but remarkably
little. The full story of why this happened can best be told
in the next edition of this little history of Wilton Park
after talking with a broad sampling of the Germans who
were there. In the meantime the outlines of an answer
seem to emerge. Virtually all of the Germans who went to
Wilton Park could see that Hitler's brutal dictatorship
had taken their country and most of the world on a course
of terrible disaster, and they were given opportunities

to study the reasons. They could see that belief in democracy, for which Hitler had complete contempt, was
Henry Koeppler's guiding star. This made his departure
from Germany and acceptance of British citizenship a
matter of high principle rather than personal comfort
or convenience. And, above all, they could see that under
Principal Koeppler's leadership the free and democratic
way of getting at the truth was being given an honest and
thorough work-out. That won esteem, respect and ultimately, in many cases, affection.

Asked for a comment on the preceding assessment, one
of the German POWs at the very first Wilton Park session
who later went on to eminence in Germany, wrote:

> It is very fair and valid. When I came to Wilton Park
> in January 1946 it was half a year after the end of an
> awful world war, brought about by Hitler, with millions
> of dead people and chaos in many countries. We all
> had just heard the truth about the unbelievable atrocities
> committed by Germans in concentration camps. In
> occupied Germany the British troops had strict orders
> of 'No Fraternization' with the Germans.
>
> It is against this background that we German prisoners
> of war experienced Wilton Park. What Heinz Koeppler
> did was most surprising. He gave us Germans the
> possibility to become partners. He did not 're-educate'
> us (he once said that re-education was arrogance caused
> by ignorance), he did not tell us how things ought to be
> handled in Germany, but he made us think for ourselves;
> he believed it to be 'vital' in the real sense of the word,
> that Britons and Germans should get to know and to
> understand the other fellow's point of view. I cannot
> describe the encouragement and confidence Heinz
> Koeppler and his colleagues gave to us, German
> prisoners of war, by having ministers of the British
> Crown, leading Opposition speakers, economic leaders

like Lord Beveridge, professors like Lord Lindsay of Birker and so on come and talk to and discuss with us.

Behind barbed wire one could sometimes, of course, feel discouraged and pessimistic. What was the use of Wilton Park? Our possibilities were limited and wasn't the task too big? Heinz Koeppler's conviction and humanity coped with such situations. He told us that small numbers are not necessarily a bad thing, for we have, after all, good *biblical* authority for the belief that from small seeds great results may follow.

It was this kind of attitude and understanding right from the beginning of 1946 which overcame also caution and sometimes suspicion, and let H.K. win—as you so rightly put it—our respect, esteem and very often real affection.

Another who went on to renown in Germany after being at one of the earliest Wilton Park POW sessions has written, 'Democratic behaviour patterns were practised. . . . Here we enjoyed the newly discovered democratic freedoms. . . . This thing laid the personal basis for my future. My way of thinking and acting was shaped then'.

Continuing as an all-civilian enterprise after 1 July 1948, the quarters of Wilton Park were moved from Nissen huts to somewhat more comfortable and more permanent structures on the Wilton Park manor grounds. This was done primarily to provide creature comforts more in keeping with the improving standard of living in Germany and the increasing status of the German civilians coming to Wilton Park. Along with the regular sessions, which were reduced to four weeks from the six weeks they had been during the POW days, shorter sessions were developed for German VIPs, who could not or thought they could not get away from their offices for a month, and for

German Parliamentarians and government officials. 'By 1949 we could not ask the Mayor of a major German city or the Minister of a German State to come over and live in a Nissen hut', Henry Koeppler has explained.

Starting with the Swiss, the Germans were joined by a small but increasing number of Dutch, Norwegians, Frenchmen and others from Western European countries. While Germans remained the heavily preponderant group this development reinforced the gradual shift—between mid-year 1946 and mid-year 1956—away from primary emphasis on Anglo-German relations towards European and international relations broadly conceived—a development which would have a very important effect on the future of Wilton Park.

The tutors guided these more exalted participants in Wilton Park sessions on tours to have a first hand look at some British institutions—local governments, schools, industrial plants—at work or, on occasion, to attend a civic reception, sometimes with entertaining results. Alec Glasford, a pioneer tutor and one of Wilton Park's mainstays through its first twelve years, recalls that 'a very obstinate monoglot Luxemburger refused to stay under my guidance in some Midland town we were visiting and arrived a little late for the Mayor's reception, bright pink all over, having entered the door of a Turkish bath by mistake and being forcibly put through the whole treatment without being able to explain where he wanted to go'.

There was another major upgrading of Wilton Park physically when it opened its first session at Wiston House in January 1951. The move was forced by the British Army's need, created by the Korean War, to occupy the buildings Wilton Park was using on the manor grounds near Beaconsfield. But, as will be made clear a bit later, the move proved a major good fortune in the development of Wilton Park.

**Summing up the first decade's accomplishments**

About Wilton Park's influence as a result of its first ten years, 1946–56, when almost all of the participants in its work were Germans, Helmut Schmidt, then the German Federal Minister of Defence, had this to say at the twenty-fifth anniversary Jubilee Conference:

> The twenty-five years to which Wilton Park is looking back today marks at the same time a critical period of German history and a most significant chapter in the development of Anglo–German relations. Wilton Park had its ample share in both of them. Specifically in the first decade of this quarter of a century, the rural seclusion of the South Downs gave birth to many ideas which became a political reality in Germany in the years to come. Almost a whole generation of German politicians defined their concept of and attitude towards Britain and the British on the basis of the impressions they received at Wilton Park. At a time where Anglo–German relations were under less favourable auspices than they are today, Wilton Park formed one of the links between our two nations which could be really relied upon.
>
> Historians of the future will perhaps give an account of the contribution rendered by Wilton Park to political developments in post-war Germany. I do not want to pre-empt their analysis. It might have been a 'ruse of history' that a historian such as Heinz Koeppler was called upon to work at Wilton Park just in the nick of time—or was it, rather, the artful historian who realized that his time had come to write a few letters in the book of history?[1]

1. 'New Forms of Co-operation in a United Europe', *Wilton Park Journal*, No. 26, March 1972, p. 26.

A British confirmation of this appraisal is made by Sir Frank Roberts who for a decade from 1957 to 1968 travelled extensively in West Germany, first as the United Kingdom's Permanent Representative on the North Atlantic Council and then as British Ambassador to the German Federal Republic. 'I was continually finding those who had been at Wilton Park in key government posts, particularly at the regional and local level', he has said. 'There is no doubt that Wilton Park has had an impact on the post-war development of Germany'.

# 2

## RALLYING TO MEET A CRISIS

Persuading the British Treasury that the Foreign Office should have the money to pay for Wilton Park had been quite a chronic struggle, at least from the days of its conversion into an Anglo–German civilian enterprise at mid-year 1948—a struggle in which Sir Frank Roberts played a key role in his capacity as British Deputy Under-Secretary of Foreign Affairs from 1951 to 1954.

Even so, it still came almost like a bolt from the blue when, in July 1956, the British Foreign Office announced that at the end of another year, which would provide the time to get it dismantled in an orderly way, Wilton Park would be discontinued. Bedevilled by the Suez crisis of that year and under pressure to hold down Government

D

expenditures, the primary reason for the decision, given by the Government headed by Anthony Eden, was the necessity of saving about £36 000 a year that the Foreign Office was spending to maintain Wilton Park. In a letter to Warden Koeppler of 2 August 1956, Paul Grey, Assistant Under-Secretary of State in the Foreign Office, wrote that the decision 'was reached only after a great deal of soul searching and in the light of overriding needs of economy'.

The announcement of the coming closing sent shock waves all through what had become Wilton Park's increasingly influential constituency. But nowhere was the shock more severe than in the Wilton Park Academic Council, a body of illustrious British scholars and public figures created in 1949, largely through the leadership of Lord Lindsay of Birker, who at the time was Master of Balliol College, Oxford.

Lord Lindsay and Henry Koeppler had become friends at Oxford through their common interest in German affairs. The Master of Balliol had lectured and led discussions at Wilton Park and during 1947 went from Oxford to Beaconsfield every week to conduct a seminar. He was also a consistent champion of the enterprise at the Foreign Office which was paying the bills and where a champion was sometimes needed, or anywhere else where there was such need, as there frequently was. It was his suggestion that 'Wilton Park should have an advisory group or Academic Council of eminent outsiders, to look after its interests and convince the authorities of its value'. He got the Foreign Office to accept this scheme and was pressed into becoming himself the Chairman, which he continued to be until illness stopped all of his outside commitments in the summer of 1950.[1]

1. *A. D. Lindsay*. A biography by Drusilla Scott, Basil Blackwell, Oxford, 1971. pp. 304, 305.

The role of the Academic Advisory Council, as outlined in the invitations to join it, was:

1. To link Wilton Park with the best British educational thought and practice.
2. To assure that the high standard for such important work is maintained.
3. To be ready to advise the Foreign Office on academic and educational questions arising from the work of Wilton Park.
4. To assure the standing of Wilton Park with British and German public opinion.

For the Academic Council the shock created by the Government's announcement of the decision to close Wilton Park was intensified by the fact that the Foreign Office had not consulted the Council before making the decision. This oversight constituted an added challenge not to take the decision lying down.

Immediately after the announcement of the coming closing, the Academic Council held an extraordinary meeting and led off what developed to be a most remarkable and effective life saving operation for Wilton Park. A resolution was unanimously passed, stating that:

> In the opinion of the Academic Council it will be an indefensible economy of money to throw away the established working institution as represented by Wilton Park for promoting understanding of common problems between different nations. So far from throwing this away, the Government might well consider using the machinery and experience of Wilton Park for international communication between a wider group of nations.

The Chairman of the Council, Robert Birley, who at the time was headmaster of Eton, was asked to communicate these sentiments to the Prime Minister in such words as he chose.

This he did in a letter in which he said in part:

> We think it highly significant that there is . . . every
> evidence of continued German approval and support . . .
> . . . we are convinced that there is still great need for the
> work which is carried on at Wilton Park. This is especially
> evident in Germany. Democracy in that country, as
> might be expected, has, as yet, very shallow roots . . .
> We believe that the experience of free discussion with
> British public figures and the insight given to the visitors
> into British institutions has proved a most valuable
> strengthening of the democratic spirit, and the feeling
> of solidarity with the West in Germany. . . . In fact, far
> from closing it, we urge that the Government should
> consider using the machinery and experience at Wilton
> Park for international communication between a wider
> group of nations . . . Wilton Park, we believe, should
> become an institution dealing not only with Western
> Germany, but with all the NATO (North Atlantic Treaty
> Organization) countries. . . . Simply to destroy a living
> organism, when work of the kind done there is going to
> prove so necessary in a larger field, would seem to us to
> be destroying a most valuable asset, one that had fully
> proved its worth.

In his letter to the Prime Minister, written on 25 July
1956, only a day after the Council had been informed of
the decision to close it,[1] Robert Birley also noted that

1. On 24 July 1956, the membership of the Academic Council included
   Dr Robert Birley, Headmaster of Eton as Chairman; Lord Beveridge,
   designer of the British Welfare State; Sir Robert Ensor, leading lecturer
   and political journalist; Dr E. Green, Chairman of one of Britain's
   foremost organizations for adult education; Professor Headlam-
   Morley, holder of the Chair for International Relations at Oxford
   University; Lord Aberdare, a peer particularly concerned with international affairs; Professor Denis Brogan, historian and journalist,
   noted interpreter of the British to Americans and *vice versa*; Sir Harold
   Nicolson, eminent writer and authority on diplomacy and politics;
   and the Rt. Rev. The Lord Bishop of Sheffield, an outstanding leader
   in the ecumenical movement.

Wilton Park, displaying 'remarkable flexibility', was already developing along the lines of broader participation in its work which he proposed. 'At the session at Wilton Park which begins today', he wrote, 'there will be present among the members M. Legendre, the head of the German section at the Quai d'Orsay, three members of the French Chamber of Deputies, two of them *anciens ministres*, and one or two directors of the *Ecole Nationale d'Adminis-tration*.

To give the effort to save Wilton Park the time required for a broad mobilization of support for it, it was necessary to cope successfully with a problem peculiar to the govern-mental system in Great Britain. The problem was that of avoiding the asking of a question in the House of Commons about the closing of Wilton Park, which could only bring a response that the Government's decision was final and thus make futile any effort to have it reconsidered. A question about the closing was ultimately asked, but not until a life-saving campaign of most impressive pro-portions, both in Great Britain and on the continent, had been carried out.

### An imposing British rescue crew

Probably the most impressive show of support in England for the continuation of Wilton Park was made in a letter addressed to *The* (London) *Times* late in November 1956 by a group of twelve eminent leaders in British public life, expressing the 'hope that this unwise decision to close Wilton Park will be reconsidered'.

The significance of the support is perhaps best indicated by a listing of those who signed the letter and who they were:

Clement Richard Attlee, Prime Minister 1945–51 (Labour MP).

Victor Feather, Assistant Secretary 1947–60 of Trades Union Congress (TUC) (Labour).

Charles Fletcher-Cooke, MP (Conservative). Barrister-at-law, Queens Council.

Hugh Gaitskell, MP (Labour). Chancellor of the Exchequer 1950–51. Treasurer Labour Party 1954.

Joseph Grimond, MP (Liberal) for Orkney and Shetland since 1950. Leader of the Parliamentary Liberal Party 1956.

Major-General Cyril Lloyd, Chairman British Association for Commercial and Industrial Education.

Richard Goold-Adams, Assistant Editor *The Economist*, dealing with foreign affairs. A founder of the International Institute for Strategic Studies, London.

Gilbert J. M. Longden, MP (Conservative). Representative to Council of Europe 1953–54.

Gilbert Murray, Regius Professor of Greek in the University of Oxford.

H. Seton-Watson, Head of the Department of History School of Slavonic and East European Studies, University of London.

George E. Scott, Editor of *Truth*.

Rt Hon. Kenneth Younger, MP (Labour). Minister of State, Foreign Office, 1950–51. Vice Chairman, Royal Institute of International Affairs 1953–55.

The letter from this imposing group said in part:

Although an understandable measure of Government economy, this decision (to close Wilton Park) implies several things. First, it would bring to an end something of proven value to the new German democracy; 'Old Wiltonians' in the Federal Republic are now doing all in their power to keep Wilton Park open, even to the extent of offering finance . . .

Secondly, the closing would remove a valuable link between British and German opinion at the very time when confidence has been severely shaken by events in

Egypt, and when it was never more important to consolidate western unity in the face of the sharp changes and convulsions which are now taking place in Russian policy. Certainly it is a false economy to increase British propaganda to the Middle East at the expense of reducing our ability to explain ourselves to our allies in Europe.

Thirdly, if this very successful institution is closed now, a great opportunity will be missed to widen its scope so that others in addition to Germans, may attend the courses. In recent months a few French, Dutch, Swiss and others have been there. Our view is that consideration should be given to developing this trend, so that other North Atlantic Treaty Organization countries may be included as well.

Other letters to *The Times*, deploring the decision to close Wilton Park, included one from Professor William Rose of the London School of Economics and Political Science in which he wrote, in part: 'The courses at Wilton Park, notable for their frank ventilation of views in an atmosphere warmed by the combination of discussion and hospitality which is one of the more lasting traditions of our old universities, have exerted influence on the attitude of important groups of German citizens and upon individuals which cannot yet be estimated. . . . The Exchequer may save £36 000 a year, but we shall have lost a continuing opportunity for studying German ways of thought and feeling such as is to be found nowhere else, not even in our universities'.

### Support for Wilton Park from the Continent

The British efforts to save Wilton Park were matched by widespread and strenuous efforts in Germany directed to the same end. In all but one of the ten *Länder* (States) of the German Federal Republic men and women who had been to Wilton Park formed groups not only to plead for its continuation, but to seek financial support that would help to make this possible. The Ambassador to London from the German Federal Republic urged the German Foreign Office to come forward with an offer of financial help for Wilton Park. Moves were made to have financial support provided either by the Federal Parliament or by the Parliaments of the States. A proposal, supported by all parties in the Parliament of Bavaria, called for an effort to obtain financial support from the Federal Government and, if this failed, to approach all of the other States with the proposal that they provide support for Wilton Park in their own budgets. Writing to the (London) *Daily Telegraph* from Düsseldorf, Germany, Lilo Milchsack, the founder of the annual Anglo–German conferences at Koenigswinter, characterized the effort 'to find public funds with which to finance the fare and stay of German participants in the future' as 'a modest gesture of gratitude for the generous hospitality received from the British Government in the past, in the firm conviction that Wilton Park still has an important mission to perform in the future'.[1]

On the London end of the Anglo–German campaign to save Wilton Park, Richard Goold-Adams, who was very active in the campaign, remarked in a letter to the (London) *Sunday Times* that 'I am surprised that more has not been made of the astounding fact that the Germans themselves are trying to raise £12 000 to prevent the closing of Wilton. Surely this is a remarkable tribute to it—which I can endorse from personal experience'.[2]

Among other Europeans hurrying to try to rescue Wilton Park, the Swiss, who had been there since the beginning of civilian participation, took a vigorous lead. They not

1. Letter to the (London) *Daily Telegraph*, 10 December 1956.
2. Letter to the (London) *Sunday Times*, 11 November 1956.

only made arrangements that would relieve the financial burdens of Wilton Park, so far as Swiss participation was concerned, but leaders of the *Schweizer Vortragsdienst* (Swiss Lecture Bureau), the organization delegated by the Swiss Government to select Swiss participants in the Wilton Park sessions, sent representatives to Germany to discuss possible steps to keep Wilton Park from dying.

This move for German–Swiss collaboration in trying to save Wilton Park was a reflection of the notably healing role it had played in post-Second World War relations between Switzerland and Germany. As one Swiss who participated in the sessions when civilians first came to Wilton Park has put it, 'At the end of the war our relations with Germany could scarcely have been worse. Wilton Park gave us an opportunity to discuss these relations in a friendly and relaxed atmosphere and thus contributed in a major way to making them better'. By virtue of their neutrality during the war the Swiss were also, on occasion, able to contribute a valuable mediating element to the Wilton Park sessions. Of these sessions Edmund Richner, the editor of the *Neue Züricher Zeitung*, who had participated in one of them, had written, 'It is political education in the best and highest possible sense'.[1]

In France, where both the number of the participants in the Wilton Park sessions and their importance in international affairs had been increased, there were numerous initiatives to encourage continuation of the sessions. And this was also true in other Western European countries, including the Netherlands and Norway, which had shared in the enterprise.

The French effort to save Wilton Park was encouraged by an article on 'Wilton Park Conferences' by René Servoise, a conference participant, which was published in *Le Monde* in August 1956 during the life-saving effort.

1. 'Wilton Park—A Bridge Between Two Nations', by Edmund Richner, *Swiss Review of World Affairs*, October 1952, p. 22.

M. Servoise urged greater French participation at Wilton Park and wrote in part, 'The directing staff of Wilton Park seem particularly conscious of the fact that lasting peaceful relations in Europe cannot be established on the sole basis of Anglo–German dialogue. We are equally aware in France that the Paris–Berlin road must necessarily pass through London. That the British are no less convinced that the London–Berlin road passes through Paris and that this manifest truth is repeatedly brought to the notice of the many participants in Wilton Park Conferences cannot but impress the French observer'.[1]

1. *Le Monde*, 8 August 1956.

# 3

# A NEW AND BROADER
# LEASE ON LIFE

Responding to what, relative to the modest size of the
undertaking, was a tremendous outpouring of support
for Wilton Park, the British Cabinet announced just
before Easter in 1957 that it would be continued for at
least another year. 'The great decision has been made',
Henry Koeppler wrote in a letter on 16 May 1957, 'Wilton
Park is to be continued'.

As had been initially suggested by the Wilton Park
Academic Council, however, it was provided that the
preponderantly German participation would give way
to a much broader international participation. Membership in the Organization for European Economic Co-
operation, which had been formed in 1948, was to be

made the basis for issuing invitations to Wilton Park
conferences, and invitations would also be extended to the
United States and Canada, which had been closely associated with the work of the OEEC since 1950. The OEEC
countries rather than the member countries of the North
Atlantic Treaty Organization, initially suggested by the
Academic Council as the countries to which invitations
to the Wilton Park conferences might be issued, were
chosen because they constituted a larger group and perhaps
particularly because they included Switzerland which had
co-operated most effectively in the work at Wilton Park
from its very beginnings at Beaconsfield. In 1957 the
seventeen member countries of the OEEC were:

| | | |
|---|---|---|
| Austria | Iceland | Portugal |
| Belgium | Ireland | Sweden |
| Denmark | Italy | Switzerland |
| France | Luxembourg | Turkey |
| Germany | The Netherlands | United Kingdom |
| Greece | Norway | |

Invitations would also be issued to other countries
as they became members of the OEEC, as Spain did in
1959, or members of what in 1960 became its successor
organization, the Organization for Economic Cooperation
and Development. Full memberships in this organization
were accorded to Canada and the United States in 1960,
to Japan in 1964, to Finland in 1969 and to Australia,
the twenty-third country to attain full membership, in 1971.
An invitation to participate in the Wilton Park conferences would also be extended to Yugoslavia, which since
1955 had been accorded special status as an observer
of the meetings of the OEEC Council and as a full
member of the organization in dealing with agricultural
matters.

For Wilton Park, as a broadly based international
undertaking, Warden Koeppler proposed to have eight
courses or conferences of three weeks each year, for which

the participants would be expected to finance their own travel and pay a fee of £10 a week; since increased to £20.

An assured lease on life for no more than one year was hardly the basis for satisfactory operations at Wilton Park, particularly in terms of job security for members of what perforce was a remarkably gifted staff. The Academic Council, reconstituted to take account of the broader international base of operations,[1] with Robert Birley continuing as Chairman, would be addressing itself to this problem. But to have Wilton Park continued at all, after the British government had announced the decision to close it, was a notable tribute to the esteem in which it had come to be held.

In the written records of the efforts to keep Wilton Park alive there is almost no mention of the part that Henry Koeppler played in them. It would be naïve, however, to believe that he, who had been characterized as 'a human dynamo' by one of his tutors, suddenly assumed a posture of suspended animation when the coming closing was announced, and stood by quietly to see if his child would be saved. With one notable exception, however, the story of what he did, beyond cataloguing the life-saving efforts of others, must await telling by those with whom he worked rather than the written record—perhaps a recognition of his philosophical observation that those who assume

1. Besides Dr Birley, the membership of the New Academic Council included Sir William Hayter, Warden of New College, Oxford and at one time British Ambassador to Moscow; Professor Max Beloff, historian, All Souls College, Oxford; Professor Denis Brogan; Viscount Davidson, party chief of the British Conservative Party; F. W. Deakin, Warden of St Anthony's College, Oxford and key British collaborator with Marshall Tito during the Second World War; Lord Harvey of Tasburgh, former British Ambassador to France; Professor A. Headlam-Morley; the Rt. Rev. Leslie B. Hunter; Professor Bernard Lewis, specialist in Middle and Near-Eastern Affairs at the University of London; Mr D. H. McLachlan, an editor of the (London) *Sunday Telegraph*; Sir Harold Nicolson; Mr Peter Tennant, Deputy Director of the Confederation of British Industry; and Mr A. W. Allen, Member of the General Council of the British Trade Union Congress.

conspicuous roles as heroes rarely thrive in governmental bureaucracies of which, Wilton Park, in its way, was one.

The notable exception is a memorandum which Warden Koeppler wrote to Robert Birley late in 1956 describing 'the specific Wilton Park formula' when efforts to assure continued use of the formula were underway. Since the memorandum provides something of an explanation of what was done during the Anglo–German period of Wilton Park, as well as a link to what would be done in the broader, international role which it was proposed that Wilton Park assume, it is quoted in full:

Four ingredients appear to me to make up the specific Wilton Park formula; the first is the mixture of all influential sectors in the community which form the membership of its sessions. Of course, it is a good thing when members of some professional group from different countries come together to talk about their common professional problems. One must, however, be careful not to indulge in the illusion that such gatherings improve the international atmosphere at the political level. Thus, to have representatives of different social and economic interests together in one session makes for greater political realism by cutting out professional 'shop'; and it increases the practical use of their meeting in making an impact on the whole public opinion of their country.

The second is the curriculum, which concentrates on the discussion of those problems which have created difficulties in the past between our nations; on establishing the causes of misunderstanding, and on helping to remove them. Such difficult tasks can only be achieved in frank discussions in which people are not afraid of telling each other what they believe to be the truth. If the free peoples are to pursue their joint interests jointly, they must understand first where the interests of each of them lie.

The third is the method of work which, while not neglecting visits to institutions which are typical of Britain to-day, centres in discussions in small groups. This alone prevents the false impressions inseparable from the usual short visit which is all that important people can find time for today.

Finally, Wilton Park has not shut its eyes to the fact, however incomprehensible it may appear to some of us, that even the leaders of public opinion abroad cannot be expected to speak and understand English well enough for serious discussion.

This last consideration may make it appear difficult to extend the work of Wilton Park beyond the Anglo–German framework in which it started. However, some progress has already been made in this direction by the increasing participation of people from other countries. French has been made an equal medium with English and German. There will be difficulties in adapting the procedure of Wilton Park work to the use of the third language but they can be overcome. It should be possible with the help of those three languages to serve a 'European' or 'Atlantic' membership of Wilton Park sessions.

**The essence of this institution is academic freedom**

In his first formal description of 'The New Wilton Park', presented in the *Wilton Park Journal* for December 1958, Warden Koeppler stressed what had been and would continue to be one of its key and most remarkable ingredients. This was the academic freedom prevailing at Wilton Park in spite of the fact that the British Government, via the Foreign Office, had been paying and would continue to pay most of the cost of the undertaking. This aspect of Wilton Park impressed and continues to impress visitors from foreign lands, and perhaps particularly those from the United States, as bordering on the miraculous.

Of the academic freedom at Wilton Park the Warden subsequently wrote:

> Most countries have a proverb equivalent to the English 'He who pays the piper calls the tune.' The British Government, through the Foreign Office, pays for Wilton Park. Does it call the tune? Yes and no. The Foreign Office have set our tasks. One of these is to make the Wilton Park conferences a British contribution to western solidarity by providing a platform for the free and frank exchange of views on vital international issues, however contentious and sensitive they may be. The other is for Wilton Park to ensure the presentation of a true and adequate picture of British policy ... Britain is still an unknown island for many people, even if they are leaders in their own countries, and what we discuss and the way in which we discuss it presents an introduction to the British way of life ...
>
> The essence of this institution is its academic freedom. And here the Foreign Office does not call the tune; on the contrary, it has imposed on itself a self-denying ordinance. We receive no directives on what issues we should discuss, nor who should be asked to come and speak here. This academic freedom, symbolically expressed in our crest, is indeed the only possible basis for our work. Our members would not be interested in a guided missile. Thus, it is not high-minded idealism but down-to-earth enlightened self-interest which has given us this precious privilege ... the keystone of our success.[1]

As a further buttress to Wilton Park's academic freedom by the Foreign Office, Warden Koeppler also reported in

1. 'Working at Wilton Park', *Wilton Park Journal,* January, 1966; p. 12.

Lord Soulbury's audience of German POWs for a lecture on 'British Institutions' at Wilton Park, Beaconsfield.

Wiston House and the Chanctonbury Ring.

Wilton Park plenary session in the lecture hall with equipment for simultaneous interpretatio

his first description of 'The New Wilton Park' that 'the Foreign Office agrees to, and indeed asks for, the maintenance of our academic independance by inviting what one may very justifiably call a very distinguished group of British citizens to form our Academic Council'. He also reported the creation of a new body, the International Advisory Council, to be composed of the Ambassadors in London of the participating OEEC countries. 'Their purpose', he wrote, 'will be to keep their own nations informed of our work and our development, to help with both, and, in particular, to advise on the best methods for the selection machinery for the new Wilton Park'.

The proposal that there be an International Advisory Council, to meet twice a year, had been put forward by representatives of the governments of France, West Germany and the Netherlands, and supported, in part, by what seems a rather far fetched appeal to the principle of 'no taxation without representation'. Henceforth participants in the Wilton Park conferences would be 'taxed' by being required to pay the cost of getting to them and to pay a modest fee which would cover a very minor fraction of the cost of the operation. Hence it was argued that the countries from which participants came should have representation in a body having some advisory share in the operation. When the International Advisory Council held its first meeting at the British Foreign Office in London, in June 1959, eight ambassadors availed themselves of this opportunity. This number had doubled when Wilton Park celebrated its twenty-fifth anniversary twelve years later—an index of a sort of growing appreciation of the importance of Wilton Park.

Largely because of the problems involved in shifting to a much broader international base of participation, the length of Wilton Park conferences was reduced to fourteen days, with ten conferences a year to be scheduled. Also, each conference was to have a 'special aspect'. This arrangement

E

was made to accommodate the unwillingness of the French government to send representatives to a conference that did not have such a specific subject for discussion. It would develop that this requirement could be met by having a subject about as broad as relations between the earth and the cosmos, but still specific. That the French governmental insistence on having a specific conference title does not reflect a rigid French cast of mind is demonstrated at the meetings of the French-speaking 'Old Wiltonians'. They have been known to gather for a meeting and to make the first order of business a discussion of what they would like to discuss.

**Ranging over wide terrain**

The wide range over which the discussion at a Wilton Park conference can range and still stay on the assigned subject is indicated by the following sampling of the subjects of conferences during recent years: the present state of East–West relations; public opinion and foreign affairs: the role of Governments, Parliaments and the mass media; protest and dissent in the Affluent Society; problems of higher education; Party politics and parliamentary power; the Civil Service and the citizen; problems of democratic control; social and economic policy and its impact on the educationsal system; interdependence and competition within the West in the fields of politics, defence and economics.

Sometimes the conference subjects, such as 'The Unification of Europe: a Balance Sheet', or 'The Ameriican Challenge—its Impact on European Economics and Society', are a bit more limited. But all of them intentionally provide leeway for far ranging discussion.

Conference subjects also explicitly include defence, in all of its military, political, social and economic aspects. This is frequently regarded as much too prickly a subject to lend itself to a tolerably comfortable international conference. Indeed, when the subject was first introduced at Wilton Park one of the conference members complained that he had come to improve international understanding and not to discuss such a divisive subject as defence. Warden Koeppler maintained and continues to maintain however, that one lane of the road toward more peace and better international understanding is more knowledge of the mainsprings and manifestations of arrangements for defence. So there have been Wilton Park conferences on such subjects as: economic and political aspects of Atlantic Defence; aid and defence—priorities and problems; priorities in Western Defence—European, Atlantic and Pacific.

To cope as effectively as possible with the language problems introduced by the broader international participation in the Wilton Park conferences, equipment for simultaneous translation in German, French, and English was installed for use at the general or plenary conference sessions. The conference programmes were also printed in these languages. And starting with the issue of December 1958, the semi-annual *Wilton Park Journal* was and continues to be published in English, French, and German.

The programme and physical changes made at Wilton Park with its conversion from an essentially Anglo–German to a much broader international enterprise provided the basic design for its operations, which has since been maintained. There have been a few additions to the programme and, of course, a large increase in the breadth of the international participation. But the format for the Wilton Park conferences, outlined for Sir Robert Birley by Warden Koeppler, has remained basically the same. The principal change has been increased competence in applying the formula to an increasingly urgent set of international problems.

There was some modification in the schedule of ten two-week conferences a year which the Warden initially proposed when Wilton Park was converted into a broadly international enterprise in 1957. Two of the ten conferences were reduced from two weeks to a single week. In 1971 there was experimentation with a sort of hybrid conference where the participants would have the option after one week of staying all or part of a second week, but this arrangement was soon dropped. So the standard Wilton Park conference menu is eight two-week conferences and two one-week conferences a year.

Also in 1964 a special kind of conference, unlike the regular Wilton Park conference in the nature of its participants, was added to the schedule which had been initially proposed by the Warden. It was that of an annual diplomats' weekend conference. This was initially suggested by the Norwegian Ambassador to the Court of St James, HE, Mr Arne Skaug, who at the time was Chairman of the International Advisory Committee, a post rotated annually among the ambassadorial members of the Council. He told his Council colleagues that the members of the staffs of the embassies in London rarely had an opportunity to meet each other and their opposite numbers in the British Foreign Office to discuss matters of general interest in a relatively leisurely way. 'The experts on fish get together to talk about fish', he said, 'and that's all they do talk about. Fish are important, but so are a lot of broader matters they never have a comfortable opportunity to discuss with each other'. Consequently he suggested that a weekend conference at Wilton Park, perhaps at the Counsellor or First Secretary level in the embassy hierarchy, would provide the opportunity for such discussion. Members of the Council and the Foreign Office agreed, and the first diplomats' conference, limited to members of the embassy staffs of western world countries which were members of the OECD was held in the fall of 1964. In 1967 and again in 1970 and 1971 the diplomats' conference was broadened to include members from

embassies of eastern European countries. With one exception, the inclusion of participants from Communist
countries of Eastern Europe in Wilton Park conferences
constituted a new departure. The exception was Yugoslavia,
which, by virtue of its special relations with the OECD,
had been sending participants to regular Wilton Park
Conferences since 1961, generally one at a time.

From the beginning, with the POW sessions in January
1946, there had by the end of 1972 been a total of 232
Wilton Park sessions. Of these 85 had been during the
Anglo–German period and the balance after Wilton Park
became broadly international. By a process of trial and
error, the length of the regular Wilton Park sessions had
been varied from about six weeks, as the standard during
the POW days, to two weeks for most of the contemporary
conferences.

**Taking enough time to get acquainted**

The two-week length of most of the Wilton Park conferences
is one of their distinctive features and one which rouses
some disagreement. There is the view that influential
people who should have a Wilton Park experience are also
generally very busy people and find it difficult if not impossible to take two weeks off.

One extreme statement of this viewpoint was made by
an American editor who remarked that 'I suspect that
two weeks at conferences are a luxury only to be afforded
by academics and unemployed intellectuals'.

Warden Koeppler and his colleagues on the academic
staff find, however, that a two-week conference is far more
effective than a conference of one week in generating that
frank and still genial discussion of the thorny sort of
problems that are tackled at Wilton Park, and so also do
most of the participants. In support of the longer conference the Warden has written that 'Whatever their field,
be it administration, industry, the army, the church or the

communications media, these key people, the people who carry the load, are most in danger of concentrating too much on their particular tree—either making it grow or cutting it down—and most in danger of not seeing the woods of which the tree is a part'.[1]

He finds it encouraging to his faith in the efficacy of two-week conferences that, to quote him, 'More and more the top decision-makers have come to accept that it is not just kindness or social welfare but downright efficiency to give their key people a sabbatical breather, to get away from their desks to see the change in basic factors, note new evaluations and new forces in society and in technology which, albeit indirectly, affect their own work. Asking for two weeks of men and women badly needed in their jobs made Wilton Park, in the forties and fifties, extremely suspect in the eyes of the British Treasury, so suspect that they completely ruled out participation of British officials in our conferences. Now they are actively encouraging it'.[2]

### How and what people get to Wilton Park

In selecting those to be proposed as participants in the broadly based international conferences at Wilton Park, the countries receiving regular invitations to make selections (initially the member countries of the European Organization for Economic Co-operation, Canada, the United States and Yugoslavia, and since 1961 the member countries of its successor, the Organization for Economic Co-operation of Development) follow quite different procedures. In Switzerland, a pioneer and steadily continuing participant at Wilton Park, the Swiss Parliament provides an annual appropriation for a non-governmental agency which until 1971 was the *Schweizer Vortragsdienst*

1. 'Purpose, Aims and Methods of Wilton Park', *Wilton Park Journal*, March 1972, p. 10.
2. Opening statement by Warden Koeppler at the 25th Anniversary Wilton Park Jubilee Conference, *Wilton Park Journal*, No. 46, March 1972, p. 10.

and is now the *Schweizeriches Komitee für Wilton Park unter dem Patronat des Forum Helveticum*. With the help of a group of eminent citizens active in public life, the *Komitee* proposes participants for Wilton Park and pays for their transportation and their conference registration fees. The Parliaments of Norway, Denmark, and Sweden provide money to enable their parliamentarians to go to Wilton Park. A Joint Committee of the Central Confederation of Finnish Industry and Trade Unions nominates Finns to go to Wilton Park and finances their participation. In some other European countries the nomination of participants is made directly by their Foreign Offices, sometimes in collaboration with the British Embassy in that country and sometimes in collaboration with civic, business, labour, and academic organizations.

In contrast, in the United States, from which participants have been coming in a steady and expanding stream since 1961, there is no governmental involvement in the selection process. 'Old Wiltonians' constitute the primary source of recommendations of Wilton Park participants. Participation by Americans in substantial numbers was first made possible by a "pump-priming" grant of $100 000 by the Ford Foundation to Wilton Park to pay travelling expenses for those chosen as participants who could not defray their own. Access to the grant was first limited to Americans, then extended to Canadians and subsequently to Europeans far distant from Wilton Park. The $100 000 provided by the grant was exhausted some years ago, but it has in some part been replaced by contributions from its members to the American Wilton Park alumni association, called the American Friends of Wilton Park, which are used to help pay travel expenses to Wilton Park of particularly promising American participants who could not get there otherwise.

Participation in the Wilton Park conferences has also been further stimulated by both formal and informal arrangements by several midwestern universities in the United States to help members of their staffs to get to Wilton Park. Iowa State University makes two Wilton Park Awards each year to finance participation in a Wilton Park conference by faculty members who have recently 'performed some outstanding international service in terms of teaching, research, or administration'. Although without any formal contractual arrangements, the University of Missouri makes it possible for two of its staff members to go to a Wilton Park conference each year, and it has also financed participation in seminars on one or more of its campuses by members of the Wilton Park academic staff. The Universities of Indiana and Wisconsin also have informal arrangements for co-operation with Wilton Park, as does Ohio State University.

The different methods used in different countries in selecting those to be recommended as Wilton Park participants has a marked bearing on the occupational character of the participating groups from these countries. Where governmental agencies select the prospective participants and pay their transportation and conference fares, civil servants tend to predominate. Where the selection process is non-governmental, as in Switzerland and the United States, a broader occupational band gets represented.[1]

Of about four thousand participants in Wilton Park conferences since they were put on a broad European and North Atlantic base in 1957, up toward half have been civil servants in local, regional, national, foreign service, and defence capacities, With a few notable exceptions the balance has been pretty well spread over the spectrum of occupations and professions. The exceptions are provided by those engaged in technology, science, medicine,

1. In Europe, historically at least, civil servants, defined as those paid by government, have been engaged in a wider range of occupations than is the case in the United States and Canada. Thus 'civil servant' is a quite inexact occupational classification, but a better one is not available.

agriculture, and trade union leadership, where there has been a rather consistent paucity of participation.

The age span of those who have participated in Wilton Park conferences has been very broad. It has ranged from some in their twenties to a few in their eighties. In accounting for this relatively distinctive characteristic of Wilton Park, Warden Koeppler has said, 'We mix the age groups: to a degree which I do not want to exaggerate, we counteract the so-called generation gap. I am not saying that we go from teenagers to centenarians, but we do have a median age of forty to forty-five, which embraces people of about thirty who have just ceased to belong to youth with a capital "Y". They are not here because they are young but because they are good in their specialized field. And we do include, very happily, people who have ceased their original occupation but who are still about doing much good in the world. This implies that we are not over-concerned with "status" '.[1]

Since it became broadly international in 1957, Germans have continued to provide the largest contingent of Wilton Park conference participants, about one fourth of the total. This is understandable, since it was in Germany that Wilton Park first became widely known. Although late starters—only two participated in 1958, one in 1959 and three in 1960—Americans are second only to Germans in the number of participants, now over six hundred. The balance of the participants has been spread by nationality over the member countries of the OECD regularly invited to send participants, with relatively large representation coming from some of the smaller countries in total population. There has also been a considerable number of participants from other than OECD countries and from international organizations, as is indicated by the following

1. Opening statement at the Twenty-fifth Anniversary Conference. 'Purpose Aims, and Methods of Wilton Park'. *Wilton Park Journal*, March 1972, p. 3.

detailed breakdown of participation by nationality in Wilton Park conferences between 1956 and 1971:

| | |
|---|---:|
| Germany | 1 061 |
| USA | 610 |
| UK | 462 |
| Austria | 373 |
| France | 300 |
| Italy | 296 |
| Switzerland | 294 |
| Spain | 143 |
| Norway | 139 |
| Denmark | 135 |
| Netherlands | 116 |
| Belgium | 84 |
| Sweden | 84 |
| Finland | 79 |
| Turkey | 72 |
| Canada | 32 |
| International Organizations | 27 |
| Yugoslavia | 26 |
| Luxembourg | 19 |
| Greece | 18 |
| Portugal | 17 |
| Iceland | 3 |
| Ireland | 2 |
| | |
| Non OECD countries | 35 |
| | |
| TOTAL | 4 427[1] |

1. This total includes 411 wives or husbands, as the case may be, of those formally designated as conference participants.

# 4

## SOME NOTABLE THINGS ABOUT A
## WILTON PARK CONFERENCE

When the participants in a Wilton Park conference, usually numbering between 25 and 50, arrive for what is generally a two week session, a number of unusual things happen right away. For one impressive thing, each person is warmly greeted by a member of the Wilton Park staff. There is none of the lonely wandering about, trying to find the registration booth and directions to living quarters, that blights so many conferences on both sides of the Atlantic. Welcoming new arrivals at a Wilton Park conference has been made a gracious art.

The quarters to which the participants are escorted are in a great house which, under the name of Wistanestun, is mentioned in the Domesday Book of 1086, as is the adjoining church. In almost nine centuries since then the house and its park have been owned by only four families, an average of more than 200 years per family. Most of the present house is where it was in 1576 when the original medieval house was replaced by an Elizabethan mansion. At the time the Domesday Book was compiled the original house, or fortified manor as it may have been, was owned by William de Braose, one of the most powerful of William the Conqueror's henchmen who, as a reward for his services to the king, received large grants of land in Sussex.

When John de Braose, a descendant of William, died in the middle of the fifteenth century without a male heir, Wiston passed to the Shirley family through marriage. A medieval manor house did not fit the tastes of the time, so Sir Robert Shirley had it torn down and in 1576 re-placed by an Elizabethan mansion.

The Shirley family went so heavily into debt vainly supporting the cause of Charles I that it was forced to sell Wiston. The new owner was Sir John Fagge, a member of the tribunal that tried Charles I. He refused to sign the king's death warrant and so retired, or perhaps was retired, from political life to live on his newly acquired estate.

The Fagge family lived at Wiston House until 1743 when, through marriage, it was acquired by the Goring family. This family has owned it and its park in the span of well over 200 years since. How, in the light of British tax and inheritance laws, it has managed to do this would be a fascinating study, but it is not part of this chronicle.

Very shortly after the Gorings took over there were major alterations in Wiston House, apparently completed in 1747 at the direction of Sir John Goring, the first Goring owner. The house was reduced to its present size from a much larger structure. Then about a century later the Elizabethan character of the house was drastically modified by an architect, in vogue at the time who, among other things, hired Italian plaster workers to adorn the walls of the great hall with swirls and flourishes of stucco work. To accommodate a fireplace consistent with this work, the Renaissance stone mantelpiece in the great hall was relegated to an outside wall of the house, where it is now being protected from the ravages of weather by a plastic coating.

The stables, built shortly after 1576, are the only Wiston House structures that have not been more or less drastically remodelled since. But the changes since the Elizabethan mansion was erected in 1576 have not been such as to deny Wiston House authentic classification as such.[1]

Into this Elizabethan mansion have been fitted living and sleeping quarters which preserve much of its old English dignity and also provide a substantial measure of modern comfort and convenience, extending even to the provision for the guests of an electric washing machine and dryer. Of these amenities an Italian conference participant remarked that 'the old house, like so many in Britain, is full of "comforts" which for many Europeans are very uncomfortable indeed'. There is little doubt, however, that a broadly based international poll of Wilton Park conference participants would show this judgement to be much too harsh.

As befits a house seasoned by centuries there is a Wiston House ghost. It has not been active lately but its potentialities for future enterprise add a certain element of zest to a Wilton Park conference.

The equipment for the plenary conference sessions, attended by the staff and all conference participants, includes deep upholstered armchairs which are comfortable but not soporific. There is also the somewhat magical

---

1. This brief summary of the history of Wiston House is taken from a more extensive history, copies of which are made available to participants in Wilton Park Conferences.

electronic system for simultaneous translation, which gets word from the speaker to the interpreting booths by wireless transmission. The rooms for smaller conference sessions and informal discussions include a common room of handsome proportions, with notable ornamental plaster work frieze and ceilings.

The library to which the participants are introduced, a high ceilinged room with oak panelling, decorative carvings and a great fireplace, has a small but carefully selected collection of reference books which the participants will find little time to consult. There is also a large spread of English, European and American newspapers which involves the participants in the only conference exercise which seems to have an almost ritualistic character. This is the filing into the library after breakfast to shuffle through the newspapers to make sure that no major international development has taken them unawares.

### A most controversial matter of taste

How much one enjoys the food at Wilton Park, served in the high arched great hall, with its rather unfortunate eighteenth century baroque embellishments, is apt to depend in some degree on the place from which one comes. For the French and Swiss, generally accustomed to fine food, it may be something of a trial. For the British, whose cooking has improved enormously since the Second World War, it may be no great treat. But by many and perhaps most of the conference participants it is pronounced good, is served with grace and dazzling speed and can be made easier to take, if necessary, by the individual purchase of wine or beer.

(Note: The preceding paragraph has aroused more controversy than any other in this chronicle. The slighting reference to the eighteenth-century baroque embellishments in the dining hall was challenged as reflecting a lack of artistic discrimination. 'The plaster work is the best thing in the hall. If you wish to be critical attack the roof, it is rather poor', was the diversionary tactic employed.

The suitability of making any comment at all about the food for the stomach at an establishment dedicated to enriching food for the intellect, and perhaps the soul, was questioned. And most of all, if food for the body were to be mentioned, there was vigorous contention that any rating other than excellent would be scarcely less than slanderous. One line of complaint was that it is grossly unfair to apply a *Cordon Bleu* standard to institutional food, which that at Wilton Park must be. 'As such it is wonderfully good'.

About one aspect of the food served at Wilton Park there is complete unanimity. This is that Albrecht Handerer, the chef, who had been a German prisoner of war and who came to Wilton Park in its early days at Beaconsfield to cook, is a wonderfully gracious and accommodating gentleman who, as the creator of gorgeous, calorie crammed desserts, has no superior and perhaps no peer.

How to balance out satisfactorily conflicting contentions about the food served at Wilton Park remains a major undertaking and perhaps an abiding mystery. So as a point of historical reference if nothing else, the disturbing paragraph has been left intact.)

For an initiation fee of 5p (assessed simply to comply with a law requiring payment of an entrance fee), conference participants are admitted to membership in the Chanctonbury Ring Club, tucked away in a recess of the basement of Wiston House. There the rigours of the day's work can, if necessary, be poulticed in the evening by the consumption of products of the sort purveyed by an English pub. Or a conversation, touched off by the developments of the day, can be carried into the night in a cozy and congenial atmosphere. It is unquestionably in the Chanctonbury Ring Club that some of the important progress toward international understanding at Wilton Park is made.

During the course of a conference all of the participants will, at one time or other, be invited to be guests of the Warden in his warmly hospitable 'lodgings', as he calls them, in Wiston House, there to share a meal or sherry and conversation with a visiting VIP who is at Wilton Park to lead a conference discussion. Of itself, a visit to the lodgings with their handsome panelled living room, looking out across formal gardens, and a dining room resplendent with beautiful china and glass on the table and on the sideboards makes an impressive departure from anything suggesting institutional living at Wiston House. The warmth and effervescence of the Warden's hospitality makes the break complete.

A comment on the quality of his sherry also helped on one occasion to add an element of hilarity to his hospitality. One of his American guests recalls with glee that when he complimented a secretary who had laid it out on the high quality of the sherry being served she replied in some panic, 'My God, I must have got the wrong bottle!' But it wasn't true. All the Warden's sherry is fine.

**Concentration on awkward and vital issues**

When the Warden, at the first plenary session, discusses the programme to be followed he takes an unusual course. There is a flat rejection of any sort of saccharine search for international 'togetherness' which characterizes the opening sessions of so many international conferences. As one American participant has summarized and described the conference take-off:

The Warden's opening remarks are to this effect. 'We are here not to discuss the matters that bind us together. We all appreciate that we share common tastes in music and the arts, and in other ways share a common civilization. Here we are more concerned about the matters that divide us. Talking about peace with friends gets us nowhere. (If the Russians were here it might.) Therefore in the brief time we have together let us concentrate on the awkward and vital issues that divide us. Ladies and gentlemen, in your questions please be brief, trenchant and, if possible, witty.' This straightforward, almost abrupt, greeting sets the tone of the conference.[1]

Concentration on 'the awkward and vital issues that divide us' is not limited to international affairs. It also applies to the sessions devoted to illumination of internal affairs in Great Britain—a key part of the Wilton Park curriculum from the very beginning. The discussions at these sessions are opened by leaders of public affairs in Great Britain, often members of Parliament, and of sharply differing political persuasions.

At the two-hour plenary sessions the discussion leader has about a half hour to open up the subject and generally in the process to express his point of view. The balance of the time is given over to the exchange of views. Except for not always seeing that his initial request that participants be brief is respected, Warden Koeppler has become a master in handling discussions, even to the physical arrangements involved. Standing almost six-and-a-half feet himself, and built in appropriate proportions, he enhances his command over the proceedings by using a chair inherited by Wilton Park from an English judge, which is much higher than any chair on the platform, including that assigned to the leader of the discussion.

---

1. 'Wilton Park: International Conference Champion', by William C. Rogers in the *NUEA Spectator*, Bulletin of the National University Extension Association, April–May 1969, p. 22.

F

From this imposing altitude he presides in a manner which somehow suggests a benign eagle.

With long darting gestures he spots and lines up the participants who are moved to say something or, in his odd terminology, 'to make an intervention', he bunches the 'interventions' when time is getting short, makes a running commentary on the relevance or the irrelevance of what is being said, which is sometimes quite sharp; on occasion throws in a translation of some language not covered by the simultaneous translation system; once in a while suggests the desirability of more brevity, and generally keeps the proceedings moving at a pace and in a spirit which invariably makes the time run out before the inclination to discuss the subject further has evaporated.

For each day of a conference the Warden equips himself with two roses for boutonnières, one for the morning, the other for the balance of the day, and a supply of very pungent cigars. While presiding at a plenary session, the Warden occasionally sniffs his boutonnière, (grown in his own garden) as a gentle way of suggesting that the discussion is getting a bit rancid. As for his cigars, when he sets one of them to smouldering, he turns on an exhaust fan which, while rather noisy, removes most of the smoke before it has a chance of suffocating any of the conference participants.

When Dean Robert Gibson, who spells the Warden in this role, presides at a plenary session he does not strive to make it an engaging dramatic performance, but he presides firmly and effectively. One reason for this is that he adheres strictly to one line of Wilton Park procedure which has much to do with the success of the discussions at the plenary sessions—a procedure which, if generally followed in conferences would make them much more effective. The procedure, necessitated by the fact that the machinery for simultaneous translation will handle only a single flow of speech at a time, requires that all questions and comments be funnelled through the chairman. Without placing any limitation on what may be the scope or intensity of their disagreement, no direct conversations between and confrontations by the conference participants are permitted to disorganize the discussion. They must clear their conflicts through the chairman.

Insistence on this procedure may stem, at least in part, from the POW days of Wilton Park. Then, one of the staff members of the time recalls that an exquisitely worded evening lecture on modern art, with slides, by a famous British art critic was considerably disrupted by having two POWs who were operating the slide projector getting into a furious and noisy argument as to whether one key slide was right side up or upside down.

**How it is said is illuminating**

Not only what is said by the participants about the subject at hand but how it is said is, in its way, a considerable education in one aspect of international affairs. Participants express themselves in markedly different styles. In the plenary sessions the Germans, for example, have a rather consistent tendency to speak in broad generalizations quite heavily tinctured with philosophical reflections. The French tend to speak, or at least seem to speak, in quite precise terms and also in a highly stylized manner involving an introduction to what is to be said, the saying of it, a summary of what has been said and then a conclusion. The British participants have a tendency to wander and to make their points rather casually, sometimes subtly, and usually with a trace of a smile. The Americans produce relatively little of the polished rhetoric of the Europeans, tend to be more blunt in their comments, and more interested in dealing with specific problems than in broad philosophical discussion. Knowledge of such different national styles of expression and, no doubt, the processes of thinking behind them too, is by no means a trivial avenue toward greater international understanding.

How often and how lengthily individual participants 'intervene' in the discussion depends not only on national styles of exposition but in some degree on the distribution of nationalities at any given conference. There is no attempt, or at any rate no success, at weighting conference participation to secure a balance in proportion to population, the Gross National Product or some such measure of the countries from which the participants come. Thus there may be several times as many Austrian or Scandinavian participants in a conference as there are French. In fact, relative to their population, the Scandinavian countries have provided the largest conference participation.

The plenary sessions are also sometimes enlivened and enlightened by the differing ways in which the members of the academic staff use the machinery provided for their arduous work as interpreters. Before Robert Gibson gave up his duties of interpreting as a member of the academic staff and became Dean and Chief Administrative Officer of Wilton Park in 1970, he would, on appropriate occasions, impart a wonderfully exciting and suspenseful character to his translation from German to English. 'I am waiting for the verb', he would say as a torrent of German words flowed into his ears, and then perhaps again, 'I still am waiting for the verb', and finally, 'Ah, the verb has arrived!' And then he would hurry through a polished conversion into English of what had been said.

Werner Lauermann, a member of the academic staff so skilled as an interpreter that he was a member of the very exclusive Association Internationale des Interprètes de Conférence, also had a dramatic flair that could take a flow of German words reaching him in a deadly monotone and, while staying right on the beam as an interpreter, make it seem a thrilling recital. And he could do the same thing going from English into German.

He also permitted himself an editorial comment on the discussion from time to time as, for example, in the case of an American University professor who, no matter what the subject under discussion happened to be, always devoted his 'intervention' to deploring the desperate plight of higher education in the United States. When the professor again got recognition to repeat his dirge, Werner Lauermann was heard to whisper to the interpreting machine, 'Here comes gloom and doom again', before intrepidly and faithfully discharging his interpreting duty.

What passes through the language interpreting system does not surmount all language barriers and perhaps particularly those faced or created by some Italian participants who are often eloquently and dramatically fluent in their own language but reluctant to use any of the three languages geared up for interpretation. This, on occasion, provides Warden Koeppler with an opportunity for a virtuoso performance both in Italian–English interpretation and condensation.

And, of course, the translating machinery does not of itself iron out difficulties brought about by the American English spoken by participants from the United States. But the members of the academic staff have become very adept in this branch of the art of interpreting.

Entertainment is provided from time to time by linguistic lapses. There is the merrily recalled case of the German-speaking Swiss who was so confident of his English that he elected to make his 'intervention' in that language. 'The flesh pots of the West, and the desert of the East' came out as 'the meat dishes of the West and the dessert course of the East'. A German, speaking confidently in English and wishing to identify his role as an educator, is recalled to have explained, 'I am a teacher of adultery education'. How much excitement this pedagogical identification aroused is not recorded. There is also a merry recollection of still another German participant who, being identified as a teacher, made a stern correction, 'I am not a teacher. I am a university professor'.

From its earliest days Wilton Park had the problem of coping with language barriers, sometimes with entertaining results. Alec Glasfurd, who joined the tutorial staff of Wilton Park for its very first session, and went on to a successful literary career after staying on the job for 12 years, recalls, 'The most impressive-sounding job I held in the war (though only briefly) was Acting Director of Manpower in the Fortress of Gibraltar. Encouraged by the Warden, as so many sonorous achievements were being rolled out during the introductory session of a VIP Conference, I mentioned this in self-defence. But my *stellvertretender Direktor der Manneskräfte in der Festung Gibraltar* delighted the Germans because it meant Director of 'virility'. I should have said 'Arbeitskräfte'.

From the outset it was recognized at Wilton Park that more than superficial knowledge of the language being used was essential to any truly meaningful dialogue and arrangements for interpretation were made accordingly. By way of underlining the importance of adequate interpretation, Mr Glasfurd recorded verbatim and has preserved the opening remarks of a lecturer from Spain who refused the offer of an interpreter. 'Long run problems never try to solve himself in short run', he said. 'Instead to get better will proceed to get less little. I propose that you agree with these facts.' 'The lecture', Mr Glasfurd concluded, 'went on like this for half an hour and showed how right Wilton Park was in insisting that the linguistic problem must be tackled properly if there is to be any fruitful meeting of the minds'.

At the plenary, as well as at all other sessions, members of the academic staff are free to express their personal point of view on the issue at hand, an opportunity which a member of the staff remarked gratefully is probably not extended to any other British civil servant. However, members of the academic staff are also duty bound to see that the point of view or views conflicting with their own are fully developed.

### Meeting in small groups

Between the plenary sessions the participants meet in small groups, generally of about a dozen, which may well constitute what the Warden has characterized as the 'most basic strength of the Wilton Park formula'. But they still are plagued by the weakness created by continuing language barriers. Each small group uses one of the three conference languages—German, French, and English— and the composition of the groups is governed by the participants with capacity to handle the particular language used. This results in having some concentration of nation-alities in small groups which is not true of the plenary sessions.

There is, however, no comparable concentration on what is discussed, or the range of occupations and professions doing the discussion. Drawing on their experiences with small groups, two members of the academic staff constructed this model of what might be the mix in such a group: An Austrian banker, and American university adminis-trator, a Belgian diplomat, a British businessman, a Dutch defence expert, a Finnish trade unionist, a French advocate, a German State legislator, an Italian treasury official, a Scandinavian parliamentarian, a Swiss tech-nologist and a Turkish editor.[1]

In the small groups the discussion may range as widely as the members of the groups elect to have it, so long as

1 . It has been suggested that this might be a somewhat idealized group, in terms of the capacity of people from such a diversity of nations to speak comfortably and competently in a common language.

the discussion is making a consequential contribution to fulfilling the basic Wilton Park purpose—to help in creating a broadly enlightened international public opinion. What the small groups provide, which the plenary sessions cannot provide in like degree, is the opportunity for extensive give and take among the participants on the subject at hand. They also add an important element of flexibility to the total programme.

By their informality the small groups encourage participation in the discussion by wives of those formally designated as participants, and the wives often add an important dimension to the discussion. They can, if they wish, 'intervene' in the plenary sessions, which many of them attend, but they generally do not. Women are also invited to be conference participants in their own right. And when national officers of the League of Women Voters in the United States were conference participants on this basis a number of their husbands joined them. However, the feminine element of a Wilton Park conference has been made up largely of the accompanying wives of participants. In recent years about 10 per cent of the participants have been joined by wives.

At all Wilton Park conferences the vitality of frank and honest exchange of views is strengthened by the clear understanding that the participants are expressing their views as individuals, and in no sense officially. There is no reason to doubt that some of the civil servants who participate in Wilton Park conferences write reports of their experience there for their governmental colleagues. There is no more reason to doubt this than there is to believe that a statement made 'off the record' is being dropped into a bottomless well of anonymity because of this self-protective provision. Perhaps it is merely being made a bit easier to deny having made the statement if this becomes convenient. However, the understanding that the participants at Wilton Park are speaking as individuals provides a considerable lubricant for free and frank discussion. So too does the fact that there is no call for the passing of resolutions and the reaching of conference conclusions and consensuses at the end of a session.

In the small group discussions and in fact in all sessions, there is a tabu on discourse of the sort in which specialists exchange views which have as their bounds their particular specialities. This tabu not only imposes extraordinarily exacting requirements on the members of the Wilton Park academic staff, but also gives the conferences one of their most distinctive, constructive and continuously sustained characteristics. It recently became part of the formal announcement of each conference that 'Wilton Park avoids narrow specialization' but from the beginning this was part of the basic Wilton Park design.

### Narrow specialization not welcome

At one of its earliest meetings Warden Koeppler told the Academic Council that he recognized 'a special duty to help people realize that, in a free society, being good at one's job is not enough . . . future leaders of German public opinion should not be narrow specialists only but be aware of their wider responsibilities as citizens and Europeans'. Harold Nicolson, then a member of the Council, supported this point of view with the observation that he regarded 'worship of the specialist as a national and international danger'. And Robert Birley, the Chairman of the Council, stressed the importance of 'the mixing of different German elements' in providing perspective on responsibilities of citizenship.

For the guidance of those engaged in selecting civilians to participate in the early courses at Wilton Park at Beaconsfield it had been stated: 'Wilton Park does not exist to foster the general knowledge and professional ambitions of its visitors nor merely to show them how their British counterparts perform their jobs; its function is a much wider and more urgent one, namely to make already professionally efficient persons aware of their wider social responsibilities as citizens and Europeans'.[1]

This early and continuing emphasis at Wilton Park on the avoidance of narrow specialization has struck an appreciative chord in particpants in its conferences from many different lands over the years. In support of it, Dr Heinz Pentzlin, Economic Editor of *Die Welt* (of Hamburg, Germany) wrote in 1956: 'when hockey players or horsemen from different countries meet they find no difficulty in talking sport together. The same goes for any profession and for any social or intellectual movement. All of them quickly find common ground, but their meeting has practically no further effect on the attitude and the policies of their peoples and states'.[2]

A few years later, Pierre Savini wrote in the Italian *Mondo Economico* that 'It is to be feared that the intellectual "baggage" of so-called "cultured" persons is largely composed of a solid core of knowledge garnered from their professional activity, sandwiched between two thin layers of general knowledge, residues of youthful memories of school teaching and stray items picked up on the way through life'. For this ill-balanced and undigestible sandwich he placed much of the blame on the abundance of 'horizontal' exchanges between similar specialist thoughts and ideas, while neglecting more 'vertical' exchanges between individuals of varied experience and more general and wide concept. And he expressed his appreciation to Wilton Park for providing an opportunity on a practical scale for 'those who feel that their public and personal responsibilities oblige them to devote more time to basic subjects, over and above their professional duties'. In further tribute to Wilton Park, Signor Savini wrote:

1. 'Notes for Guidance in Selection of German Personalities to Participate in Wilton Park Courses.' Wilton Park, Beaconsfield, Bucks.
2. *Die Welt* (Hamburg), 3 January 1956.

'There is no question, however delicate, difficult or contro-
versial that cannot be discussed in a reasonable, tactful
and frank way'.[1]

Expanding on the same general sentiment, G. B. J.
Hiltermann, the leading Dutch television commentator,
who at the time was Foreign Editor of *Elsevier's Weekblad*
(of Amsterdam) said of Wilton Park:

> It seems to me that it is in fact the only place where a
> completely frank exchange of opinions is possible be-
> tween academics, politicians, diplomats, civil servants
> and publicists of every kind, in a word between people
> in positions of some importance, who have some say
> in the determination of the world's future and who,
> as a rule, look upon each other with a degree of scepticism
> and indeed mistrust.[2]

**A tough assignment**

Keeping the kind of exchange described by Mr Hiltermann
on a useful course might, viewed superficially, seem a
relatively simple exercise. The nature of the exchange,
between people of diverse occupations and or professions,
calls for a relatively simple and direct method of expression,
free of the technical jargon that may at least provide a
patina of profundity for a discussion where there may be
none. Also the discussion in the small groups at Wilton
Park is allowed to take a free course, both in selection
and pursuit of the subject, where the member of the
academic staff in charge may, on occasion, offer one of the
participants the chair for the discussion leader.

Any impression that the Wilton Park academic staff
member does not have a tough job, however, is a complete
illusion. He must have or be striving toward having a

1. *Mondo Economico*, No. 4, 27 January 1962.
2. From the text of a broadcast, published in *The Wilton Park Journal*,
   No. 39, 1968.

broad knowledge and understanding of the workings of British political and social institutions as well as those of the countries which have participants in the small group discussions which he leads. He must be a master of the art of seeing that the discussion is kept both knowledgeable and broad. And to his duties is added the arduous work, already mentioned, of being an interpreter from French or German to English and vice versa. The members of the academic staff take off their coats and sweat in the simultaneous interpretation booths during their half hour tours of duty, followed by half an hour of rest, and thus provide very visible evidence of the strenuousness of the work. There is less direct physical evidence of the rigours of their work as small discussion leaders, but they exist nonetheless.

Beyond the capacity to act as a very competent French, German or English language interpreter, the widely varying experiences of the members of the academic staff before joining it at Wilton Park make it clear that there is no standard route of preparation for the post. Werner Lauermann, whose long and distinguished career as a member of the academic staff has already been cited, came out of the European labour movement. In contrast, at least of a sort, Bryan Shepherd, a member of the academic staff since 1969, came out of the British diplomatic service. After graduation from Cambridge University in 1938, followed by military service in the Second World War, his long and wide ranging career in the diplomatic service included posts of high rank in France, India, Singapore, Bulgaria, North Vietnam and Denmark.

Robert S. Sturrock, a member of the academic staff since 1959, got to Wilton Park following a career devoted in major part to teaching French, possibly with a slight trace of Scottish accent, at all levels from the elementary to the university. After earning an MA degree at Glasgow University in 1950, and subsequent studies at the University of Poitiers in France, he attained a degree of mastery

of French–English interpretation that has won him membership in the London Association of Conference Interpreters.
During his two year term of military service he lectured
at Hamburg and at NATO bases on European politics.

Oliver G. Hayward came to the Wilton Park academic
staff in 1964 from a post as Director of Studies at the
International Forum, an adult education centre in the
Black Forest of Germany which he had held for four years.
Prior to graduation from Cambridge in 1959 with an MA
degree in modern languages, he had had two years of
military service. After his graduation he spent a year and
took a diploma at the College of Europe in Bruges,
Belgium. At this post-graduate institution, the only one of
its kind, European studies cutting across national lines
are carried out by about forty students from many different
countries.

John Allen, the most recent addition to the Wilton Park
academic staff and its youngest member (he was born in
1945) came from Oxford where he had been working in
the University Registry which, in Oxford terminology,
means administration. He is a graduate of Merton College,
Oxford, where in 1966 he earned an MA in what is called
modern history, but for him was medieval history. As a
Merton College scholar, he had another quaint Oxford
title, that of Postmaster. Mr Allen had spent five early
childhood years in Germany, and had studied for a year
at the University of Munich before going to Oxford. He
also did volunteer teaching for two years in Northern
India, and was a temporary member of the Wilton Park
academic staff for five months in 1970.[1]

1. Here is an alphabetical listing of former members of the academic staff
   or tutors, as they were titled during Wilton Park's earlier days, together
   with their lengths of service in this capacity:

|  | Length of Service | |
| --- | --- | --- |
| Name | Start | Finish |
| Baird, Mr G. B. | 25 April 1960 | 18 February 1961 |
| Balfour, Mr D. | 15 September 1966 | 4 December 1968 |

continued on page 78

There are, however, certain common characteristics of successful members of the academic staff at Wilton Park, beyond their linguistic skills. One is intellectual alertness. Another is a liking for people, of all the remarkable varieties reaching Wilton Park. Another is an insatiable curiosity about the unfolding British and international scene, and a driving ambition to increase understanding of its significance. To do this effectively a combination of modesty and quiet authority is essential. So is a strong constitution to provide a physical backup for an unflagging enthusiasm for the hard work at hand.

In imparting such enthusiasm Warden Koeppler takes a contagious lead. Although he has done it well over a hundred times already, the Warden introduces each new conference with a zest and enthusiasm reflecting a conviction that he is off on a great new and thrilling adventure. 'And in fact', he says, 'each conference is a new adventure. The participants are new and bound to be interesting. The subject is new. The world has moved and we have the

*continued from page 77*

| | | |
|---|---|---|
| Beer, Mr C. G. | 24 July 1947 | 30 June 1948 |
| Cameron, Miss A. M. | January 1953 | December 1953 |
| Cowley, Mr G. Fraser | 4 April 1961 | 1 September 1962 |
| Glasfurd, Mr A. L. | 15 August 1946 | 5 July 1958 |
| Greene, Mr G. H. D. | 31 December 1945 | 31 August 1958 |
| Gross, Mr J. P. A. | 1 January 1964 | 15 September 1966 |
| Ground, Mr R. P. | 1 June 1958 | 6 May 1960 |
| Lauermann, Mr. K. W. | April 1946 | October 1971 |
| Lindsay, Mr. J. Martin | 1 January 1947 | 30 November 1950 |
| Marett, Mrs Cleaves | 1 January 1959 | 31 December 1963 |
| Montagu-Pollock, Sir William | 4 April 1964 | 31 October 1964 |
| Rose, Mr E. Michael | 1 February 1969 | 26 July 1969 |
| De Sausmarez, Mr C. | April 1951 | December 1958 |
| Winthrop-Young, Mr J. | 1 October 1962 | 31 December 1963 |

Mr Glasfurd and Mrs Marett supplemented their periods as full-time members of the academic staff by helping later as temporary staff members, and Mr F. W. Martin was borrowed from the British Foreign Office to serve as an academic staff member for a month in late 1964.

ever thrilling job of trying to keep pace with it, and hopefully keeping a little bit ahead of it, and trying to understand and explain it. How could anyone approach such
an opportunity without tremendous enthusiasm?'

Just as a Wilton Park Conference provides a strenuous
workout for the academic staff, it does the same for the
participants. Many and probably most of them live their
regular workaday lives as specialists of one kind and
another. For them it is both intellectually invigorating
and taxing to 'give thought to, and exchange views on,
the burning problems common to us all', as Warden
Koeppler puts it. And the process is not made easier
intellectually by the fact that Wilton Park provides no
simple dogmas on which to latch for possible security and
comfort. In fact it has been remarked that 'it is easier for
a fanatic to learn tolerance at Wilton Park than for a
dilettànte to find a settled faith.'

**A series of safety valves**
As a result of a long sustained process of trial and error,
however, the schedule for a Wilton Park conference has
been tailored to take account of its intellectual rigours.
The daily schedule is uncrowded, with both English
morning and afternoon tea times meticulously observed.
During the first week of a standard two-week conference
there is a break of a day for a trip by bus to London,
where there may be a guided tour of the Palace of Westminster and a luncheon in the House of Commons with
some of its Members, or some similarly pleasant and
instructive excursion into the workings of some other
important British public institution.

When a tour of the Palace of Westminster is guided
by Dean Robert Gibson, as it usually is, it is an unfor-
gettable educational and dramatic experience. The sturdy
old palace seems almost to tremble from the shock and horror
he registers when he tells of how a rip in the Woolsack

in the House of Lords, on which the Lord Chancellor eases his fundament, led to the discovery that it was stuffed 'not with wool but with nylon!' Happily, one learns later, this outrage has been rectified and the Woolsack made honest again by being stuffed with wool.

Over the week-end there is generally a two-day trip by bus away from Wilton Park which may include a visit to a university, with time arranged for the exchange of views with students and faculty members, a visit to one of the English new towns built to take the population pressure off London, or a visit to a British steel mill or manufacturing plant. There is no compulsion about the treks. Participants are free to stay at Wiston House or make such other week-end arrangements as they see fit.

These treks serve a number of purposes. They not only serve in their special way one of Wilton Park's basic purposes to increase the knowledge and understanding of British institutions by those attending the conference, but they also act as a safety valve for such pressures as may be built up during the talk sessions—a function generally much neglected by architects of conferences. And they shake up the conference participants, sometimes quite literally by bus travel on back country roads, in a way that accomplishes wonders in increasing the international exchange of ideas and opinions in a relaxed and informal way.

They also have potentialities for contributing to general historical enlightenment. This was the case, for example, during a visit to Hampton Court Palace which moved a Roman Catholic priest from the United States to eloquent indignation about what an outrage it had been for an English king to build such a magnificent palace while many of the common people in his realm lived in desperate squalor. This afforded a member of the Wilton Park academic staff, doubling as a guide, both an opportunity and an obligation to remind the priest quietly that Hampton

Court had been built by Cardinal Wolsey as his private residence.

### The lucky choice of Wiston House

The function of a safety valve for pressures built up during the talk sessions at Wilton Park is also provided by the spacious and venerable halls of Wiston House itself, its beautiful gardens and its setting in a great park where cattle and a horse or two grazing lazily contribute a comfortably relaxed element to the scene. It is a scene far enough removed from metropolitan distractions to discourage the seeking of surcease from the strenuous intellectual life at Wilton Park.

The location of Wilton Park at Wiston House seems to have been more a matter of good luck than meticulous planning. It was necessary to vacate the quarters near Beaconsfield. Wiston House had been vacated by an exclusive girls' school, popularly known by the unglamorous name of 'The Monkey Club' which had moved to London. This name symbolized that trio of wise monkeys that see, hear and speak no evil, and thus provide what was regarded as an excellent set of objectives for the education of young ladies. Immediately prior to housing 'The Monkey Club' Wiston House had been used as military headquarters at one time by General Bernard Montgomery, later Field Marshal Lord Montgomery of Alamein, in making preparations for a German invasion that never eventuated, and later by a unit of the Canadian Army through the time of the ill-fated Dieppe raid.

It is rumoured that one of the most distinctive works of art in Wiston House is a large 'pin-up' hung by Canadian soldiers and now hidden behind a copy of a sober seventeenth century portrait. Conference participants are not encouraged to search out the 'pin-up' although, in its way, it may have something significant to say about changes in aesthetic tastes over the centuries. It would

G

not, however, reflect the fact that the present owner of
Wiston House, Mr John Goring, recalls that 'Far the
best tenants were the Canadian Saskatoon Light Infantry
who, except for a taste for venison [there were deer in
Wiston Park] maintained the house and grounds as if
they had been their own'. Wiston House was turned up by
an estate agent as a possible seat for Wilton Park, and the
move was made there rather than to Rushbrooke Hall
in Suffolk, one of the few places that might have been
available, primarily because Wiston House was nearer
London, about fifty miles away.

In the view of most of the members of the staff, and
virtually all of the participants, however, the most pains-
taking committee on search for a home for Wilton Park
would have been very lucky to come up with anything as
remarkably satisfactory as Wiston House has proved to be.
One staff member who demurs somewhat from this view
has had part of the job of coping with its heating and
plumbing problems. Quite a number of these were involved
with equipping an Elizabethan manor house with modern
facilities of this sort, but they have gradually been sur-
mounted.

As trips away from Wilton Park provide pressure
relieving interludes for its conference participants, so
relatively frequent trips overseas between sessions or on
leave probably accomplish something of the same purpose
for the Warden and the members of the academic staff.
But these trips are also working operations, involving
particularly participation in meetings of alumni associations
of 'Old Wiltonians'. During the past decade Warden
Koeppler has had tours of duty of a semester as a Professor
of Political Science at Heidelberg University, Germany;
Visiting Distinguished Professor at Ohio State University,
USA; and Visiting Professor of West European Studies
and Government at Indiana University, USA. But a
major part of his activity abroad has been in meeting

the alumni of Wilton Park on both sides of the Atlantic. This has also been the case with the travels abroad of the other members of the Wilton Park academic staff, who have used these travels to deliver lectures and to keep the languages they use as interpreters in good tune.

**Nothing casual about the planning**

The conferences at Wilton Park typically unfold so comfortably and casually that it might be suspected that the planning of them is done in the same way. Nothing could be further from the fact. There is an extended planning session of the academic staff before each conference. There is a review of the day's proceedings on every day of the conference, directed to ironing out any kinks that may have developed or might develop. And at the end of each conference there is an extended review of the enterprise for which the members of the academic staff submit observations in writing. At these sessions there is an occasional reminder that it was not for nothing that the Warden was born and spent some formative years in what at the time was Prussia, and there picked up some of the impressive driving force that persists in him. But it is not a reminder that detracts from the pervasive spirit of co-operation and mutual good will characterizing the planning and review sessions.

In the observations of the members of the academic staff, submitted at the review sessions, there is a recurring theme. It is that reflecting a determination not to let specialists get the upper hand in the conference discussions and turn it to the narrow channels they cultivate professionally. One such observation that runs a bit in riddles is that 'The specialists are always with us, attempting to interpret "specially" the most general special subject'. 'We have', writes another member of the academic staff, 'to find a foolproof way to make clear Wilton Park's universalism, and the role of the special subject within the general framework'.

Sometimes in the observations there is an urgent appeal for a change in some part of the Wilton Park programme as, for example, the successful admonition that 'whoever is going to organize this extra-mural visit must at all costs resist any demands for more cathedrals to be included in the itinerary'. And sometimes there is an indication of the complicated and entertaining course the arranging of a round table performance by a group of Wilton Park conference participants, always a part of each conference, can sometimes take. Here is the report of one such course: 'I must preserve for the record the Saga of the International Round Table. It became a major affair of state. The four French, having been offered the session, refused after lengthy consideration and suggested a Franco–German session. The Germans went into a huddle and decided to refuse to act as *Hilfstruppen*. ("We don't want an axis Paris–Bonn; we have rather unhappy memories of an axis.") They wanted five of the OECD countries represented at the conference to form an International Round Table, and nominated one of themselves as their participant. The French nominated one of theirs, the Italians one of theirs and the solitary Belgian and Dutchman were then approached. A preliminary meeting, meant to be short and simply to settle practical points, turned into a lengthy discussion of substance and an endless procedural wrangle. . . . By an amazing feat of pursuasion, the Belgian then managed to get a full fledged talk in plenary session for himself. But as the talk was quite good and the subsequent discussion rather fruitful, I was left less with anger than amazement.'

# 5

# SOME COST AND BENEFIT
# ANALYSIS

From its very beginnings Wilton Park has forged extraordinarily abiding ties with those who have shared its work. Account has already been taken of the numerous groups of 'Old Wiltonians' in Germany which include many who date their association back to the days when the student body was composed either exclusively or predominantly of German prisoners of war and when the sessions lasted six weeks. When Wilton Park was faced with extinction in 1956 groups all over Germany rallied to its support.

Quite as remarkable in their way are the newer alumni associations which have been formed since the Wilton Park conferences were put on a broadly international basis and generally limited to two weeks in length. In Europe these newer alumni associations of 'Friends of Wilton Park', as they are commonly called, are now organized on a linguistic basis. There is the *Société International des Amis de Wilton Park de Langue Française*, centred in Paris with branches in Geneva and Brussels and there is the *Verein zur Förderung von Wilton Park, E.V.*, which centres its operations in Munich, Germany, and covers all of German-speaking Western Europe.

In the United States, a country which has fewer language barriers than Europe, at least those of which its citizens are aware, the American Friends of Wilton Park are organized on a national basis, with nine regional groups spread across the country. The Canadian Friends of Wilton Park, the newest of the alumni associations, launched in 1970, is also a national organization.

**Labours of alumni associations**

In countries where there are not enough alumni of Wilton Park to make an organization of them feasible, individuals who have been to Wilton Park serve as alumni representatives. There are now such representatives in Austria, Belgium, Denmark, Finland, Italy, the Netherlands, Norway, Spain, Sweden, and Turkey.

There are two activities that are common to all of the 'Friends'. One is seeing that men and women having a valuable contribution to give and receive by participation in the work at Wilton Park are encouraged to attend. The other activity is the extension, at meetings of the alumni groups, of the type of discussions and intellectual and social companionship experienced at Wilton Park Conferences.

In Europe there are periodic reunions of French speaking 'Old Wiltonians' in Paris, Geneva, Brussels, Liège and other French-speaking cities. Every other year week-end meetings of German speaking Wilton Park alumni are organized by the Swiss, Austrians, and Germans in their respective countries. At these gatherings the host country is represented by the Foreign Minister, the Secretary of State or some similarly imposing official.

In addition to holding reunions from time to time, the members of the Wilton Park alumni associations in North America tax themselves to help finance travel to Wilton Park by particularly promising participants who could not get there otherwise. Some financing of this sort is also provided by the French-speaking 'Friends of Wilton Park'. But the problem involved is less pronounced in Europe where governments often provide the funds to pay the travel expenses and registration fees of participants, and where the distances to travel are not so great as they are from North America.

Something of the importance that the American Friends of Wilton Park attach to helping stimulate distinguished American participation in its conferences is indicated by a twenty-fifth birthday present to Wilton Park. It is a handsomely illuminated scroll, presented on 20 June 1971 by Mr Clark Maser, then president of the American Friends, which reads:

## A TRIBUTE TO WILTON PARK

On the occasion of the Twenty-fifth Anniversary of the establishment of the Wilton Park Conferences, where scholarship and fellowship have combined to advance the great goal of North Atlantic Community, The American Friends of Wilton Park wish to express their gratitude and appreciation.

In this setting—so evocative of the common heritage and ideals shared by the peoples of the North Atlantic World—reasoned and candid dialogue has demonstrated that our problems, perils, and destiny are inseparable.

May this Community swiftly grow, a generous and responsive partner in the World Community, and may Wilton Park flourish as its companion.

The gift of the scroll was supplemented by the gift of a collection of books by American authors, regarded by its selectors as particularly relevant to the work of Wilton Park. Twenty-fifth anniversary gifts also included a beautiful silver replica of a Viking ship which bears greetings 'from grateful Norwegian Wiltonians', and was presented in person by the Norwegian Ambassador to Britain. From Spain there was a collection of essays inspired by participation in the work of Wilton Park.

What is the explanation for the success of Wilton Park in developing such loyal and enthusiastic alumni bodies of those who have been associated with it so briefly? Unless preceding observations have been peculiarly opaque much of the explanation has already been provided. But perhaps a bit of amplification is in order.

The key part of the explanation, of course, is to be found in the character of the Warden, Henry Koeppler. His enthusiasm about Wilton Park is not only contagious but he manages to make it chronically contagious, as he did in remarkable degree when his student body was composed entirely of German prisoners of war. One of the small but perhaps symbolically significant ways in which he does this is to have an old school tie for those who have been at Wilton Park. It is navy blue with the Wilton Park coat of arms, of which *Die Bruecke* is a central element, providing a pattern in gold. If the Warden were a musician there is no doubt that he would have composed a Wilton Park Alma Mater song, and there is also no doubt that those who attend the gala dinner with which each conference is closed would be singing it with enthusiasm.

There is also a Wilton Park shield designed by the

Warden. Its colour scheme embodies the colors flown by all three of Britain's major political parties south of the Trent River (i.e. in Southern England)—blue by the Conservatives, red by the Labourites and gold-yellow by the Liberals—as symbolic of Wilton Park's non-partizanship and its concern with politics. The design also incorporates *Die Bruecke* and as a symbol of freedom, and perhaps purity, the lily of Magdalen College where much of the inspiration for the bridge originated. The fact that the bridge portrayed by the shield reminded Prince Philip, the Duke of Edinburgh, of a cricket wicket and reminds others of a Roman aqueduct does not detract at least very much, from its symbolic significance in contributing to alumni attachment to Wilton Park.

### The Warden's 'Trumpet File'

The Warden maintains what, with the verve that is typical of him, he calls the Trumpet File. It is a file bulging with individual expressions of appreciation for the experience provided by participation in a Wilton Park conference. Here is a small sampling of contributions to this file:

*From the Dean of an American University:* I learned more about international relations in two weeks at Wilton Park than I had in two previous year-long tours at the American Embassy (London) and the American Embassy (Prague).

*From a Swiss Parliamentarian:* Wilton Park is not a playground for 'cold warriors' but a genuine forum and true meeting place of free people from free countries: it is a place where one not only thinks but also learns to think and go on thinking.

*From a member of the German Federal Parliament:* I am particularly grateful that we were able to discuss any problem—even the really hot potatoes.

*From an international lawyer:* At Wiston House I have found, in a way never before encountered, the free comradeship of men of different minds and national backgrounds welcoming differing attitudes, strongly maintaining their own points of view and yet acknowledging the opposition with entire grace.

*From an American corporation executive:* Nowhere else that I know of is there a forum where one may come to terms with political ideas and test reactions in a 'laboratory situation', publicly or privately, as one may at Wilton Park.

*From a French lawyer:* Wilton Park is a melting pot where prejudices and preconceived ideas dissolve and give way to a pragmatic view of the world, more realistic because it is more multinational.

*From a British Treasury official:* It came near to providing me with a new outlook—almost a new dimension—on international problems, without, I think, teaching me very much factually, which makes it the more remarkable.

*From a member of a French Military Commission:* At Wilton Park the clash of ideas cannot fail to produce something positive for every man of good faith, and without any undue selfconsciousness let me freely admit that my point of view on certain problems underwent a change.

*From a British civil servant:* I am not sure that I learned anything new but I certainly had my prejudices dented.

*From an American specialist in international relations:* There is a certain type of social chemistry which occurs at Wilton Park. Part of it, I think, is the result of the lovely location. All participants seem pleased and relaxed to be in that kind of setting, away from their routine cares and responsibilities. Conversational inhibitions therefore tend to drop away in a manner somewhat like the situation among passengers on a small ocean liner. Moreover, the Wilton Park staff is extremely skillful at this kind of chemistry, creating a personal environment where the participants are almost immediately willing to start talking to each other.

*From an officer of the British Defence Ministry:* The Wilton Park recipe seems to be uniquely successful in putting people at their ease and in provoking really frank discussion. We don't solve the problems of the world at Wilton Park but we do come to understand them more deeply and to understand each other much better.

*From a Chief of Protocol in the Danish Ministry of Foreign Affairs:* The Warden and his staff have developed political discussions to the sublime. Here is not the next best, but the best: the most crystal clear clarity.

*From an American university professor:* I returned (to the United States) convinced of the superior wisdom of any people who can contrive so effective a show case for their values as Wilton Park.

The Warden does not maintain a file of the brickbats tossed at Wilton Park by some of those who have participated in its conferences, or at least a file which he shares with others. There would be entries in such a file if it were maintained. If nothing else, the vividness of the Warden's personality, his dramatic flair and his driving force at Wilton Park are traits that do not tap wells of admiration in all of the participants. Also there is the more or less constantly recurring feeling of some of the specialists in attendance that Wilton Park doesn't really get down to the basic business, which for them may mean that it very deliberately does not give them the kind of specialists' workout which would make them comfortable.

It is clear, however, that the Trumpet File would vastly exceed in number of entries the brickbat file. One way of telling this is by reading the responses to questionnaires both about the intellectual and the physical fare provided by Wilton Park which the participants are asked to complete after each conference. The responses while perhaps slightly tinctured by politeness, are overwhelmingly favourable.

Further indicative of the esteem in which Wilton Park is held is the fact that, at one time or another a large share of the major post-war British leaders have opened discussions at Wilton Park. As previously noted, Prime Minister Heath and his predecessor as Prime Minister, Harold Wilson, have been there. So has Prince Philip. And so too have many of the public leaders of the North Atlantic Community, including Paul-Henri Spaak, Secretary General of NATO and two of his successors in that post, HE Manlie Brosio and Joseph Luns: Thorkil Kristensen, Secretary General of the OECD; Arnold Smith, Secretary General of the British Commonwealth; Jules Moch, former Premier of France; Helmut Schmidt, former Defence Minister and now Finance Minister of the German Federal Republic, whose observations at the 25th anniversary Jubilee Conference have been quoted; Theodore Heuss, former President of the Federal German Republic; Rudolph Gnaegi, President of Switzerland; Hugh D. Scott, Minority Leader of the United States Senate and Alfred Bexelius, the Ombudsman of Sweden.

Commenting on the remarkable menu offered by Wilton Park, one of the members of the academic staff, perhaps feeling a bit out of sorts at the time, wrote, 'Nowhere in the United Kingdom will the foreign visitors find an opportunity of listening to and arguing with such a collection of brilliant and authoritative representatives of various shades of British opinion. One sometimes wonders if our members fully realize how lucky they are to have such riches crammed for them into nine working days, with three excursion days judiciously sandwiched in between. Some do, others seem to take it for granted, like a good theatre or show which one has paid for and can expect to be of high standard. But do they realize that what they, or those who sponsor them, have paid is only one quarter of the market value of the goods supplied, and that the rest of the price is covered not merely by the enlightened self-interest of Her Majesty's Government, but by the personal generosity and zeal of politicians, civil servants, professors, etc.?'

### Evidence of grateful appreciation

There seems to be quite impressive evidence of grateful appreciation of Wilton Park by the participants in its conferences—in the Trumpet File, in the zestful activity of alumni associations, and in the warmth with which the Warden and other staff members are greeted by former participants when they visit them on their home grounds. How much of it can be attributed to recognition of a great financial bargain is problematical. Quite a few of the participants might think it a bit vulgar to stress this aspect of Wilton Park, just as those who open discussions at Wilton Park do not stress the fact that they are offered a standard honorarium (sometimes characterized as a fancy word for inadequate pay) in the niggardly sum of £15. The chances are, however, that while the bargain is there, it is not the recognition of it which constitutes a major component of the gratitude to Wilton Park. After all, opportunities to participate prepaid in national and international conferences of specialists abound, but they do not generate the sort of appreciation which is showered on Wilton Park. Could it be that, along with the fine hospitality in a beautiful setting, it is the nature of the discussion, which the Warden likes to describe as between a political élite of *amateurs éclairés* rather than specialists, led by members of an academic staff who are masters of their craft in an atmosphere of inspiring freedom, that constitutes a major component of gratitude to Wilton Park? There seems to be a very good chance that this is the case.

In speaking in French about the enlightened amateurs at Wilton Park, a member of the academic staff once slipped a cog and, to the merriment of his French listeners referred to them as *amateurs clarifiés* or clarified like butter. That the participants at Wilton Park neither have nor are expected to have any of this quality also adds an element of appreciation to what Wilton Park does.

When the British Government reversed its decision of July 1956 to close Wilton Park a year hence, it made a commitment, already noted, to continue it for 'at least another year'. This was obviously too short a lease on life to make possible satisfactory planning of the sessions at Wilton Park and their conduct by a staff with a tolerable amount of job security. From the outset the Wilton Park staff had had an extraordinary degree of selfless devotion to its work, perhaps particularly in the prisoner of war days, and this had served in some measure both as a substitute for salary and professional security. But having Wilton Park live on a year-to-year basis made its life much too precarious.

The Academic Council was, of course, peculiarly aware of the importance of assuring Wilton Park a more than year-to-year existence. At a meeting early in 1960 the Council agreed that it would be 'intolerable' if Wilton Park 'had to work on a year-to-year basis', and it approved a motion for 'establishing Wilton Park on at least a five-year basis in the future.'

Later in the year the Council was told by the Foreign Office that the Foreign Secretary would receive a recommendation that Wilton Park be continued until 3 March 1963, and its work reviewed about a year earlier. After that review the Foreign Office assured Wilton Park of a life tenure until March 1968, and a year before that tenure was over the Foreign Office gave assurance that Wilton

Park would be continued until March 1973. In February 1972 the British Cabinet decided on a five-year extension of life for Wilton Park, with a review to be held in 1978. Assurance was given that this time schedule carried no implication that Wilton Park would be closed in 1978.

As there had been much worry about securing a tolerable lease on life for Wilton Park, there has also been continuous concern about having enough money to make the lease at once acceptable to those giving their lives to the enterprise and also to their financial sponsor, the British Treasury.

There are many different points of view from which to assess the problem of paying for Wilton Park. It is about as difficult to bring them into a satisfactory synthesis as it is to reconcile the divergent points of view on some of the political and social problems discussed at the Wilton Park sessions.

### A most generous British contribution

In the accounting year April 1971 to March 1972 of Her Majesty's Government the total of Wilton Park expenditures was about £103 500. Of this total about £11 500 was recovered, largely in conference registration fees of about £9 000 and the rental of the Wiston House facilities between Wilton Park conferences. Thus the net cost to the Treasury of Wilton Park for the year was about £92 000.

In relation to the total expenditures of Her Majesty's Government for the 1971–72 fiscal year what was spent for Wilton Park was a small drop in the bucket. The total Government expenditure for all purposes was about £15 549 000 000. The net cost of Wilton Park of about £92 000 was about six ten-thousandths of 1 per cent, a very tiny fraction.

But viewed in the perspective of the cost *per capita* to provide the opportunity for participation in the Wilton

Park conferences, the expenditure becomes far more imposing. During the year 1971–72 Her Majesty's Government spent an average of about £20 (about 52.20 dollars or 275 French francs or 166.20 *Deutschmarks*) per day per participant in the Wilton Park conferences of that year. Viewed in this light, Wilton Park as 'a British contribution to an informed international public opinion' is a generous contribution indeed.

There is only a modest mention of this generosity of Her Majesty's Government in Wilton Park publications and no stress is put on it at the conferences. Some of the conference participants probably never become aware of it, at least in more than a vague way. When the contribution is viewed in relation to the freedom from governmental direction which Wilton Park enjoys it becomes even more impressive. Indeed to those who do their calculating in terms of direct *quid pro quo*, it is nothing less than astonishing.

As is the case with the total expenditure for Wilton Park, conclusions about the compensation of the members of the academic staff tend to be shaped by the perspective in which they are viewed. About half of the total annual gross expenditure £56 000 in 1971–72 went for salaries.

In considering the salaries of members of the academic staff, there is the point of view of the young member who some years ago discovered that his Wilton Park salary was exactly the same as that paid to the chief of a rural fire brigade in England. So he addressed a contention to the British Foreign Office that his work in putting out international fires was worthy of greater compensation than that provided for extinguishing village blazes. The Foreign Office responded by saying, in effect, that perhaps he would be more contented as a rural fire brigade chief, and did not adjust his salary upward.

One of the complications in appraising the salaries of the members of the Wilton Park academic staff in tolerably valid relative terms is that the work they do is far more exacting than that required of most college and university teachers. For one thing they must be good teachers, a requirement frequently not imposed on college and university faculty members. Warden Koeppler has emphasized the crucial importance of good teaching by ringing a change on the often heard academic mandate 'Publish or Perish' and, in public addresses, stated the real challenge to be 'Teach or Perish.'[1]

The members of the academic staff must also be expertly bilingual. And they must be able, as generalists, to range knowledgeably and perceptively over numerous fields of study which, in the standard academic establishment, are sliced into specialized segments such as those of economics, political science and sociology. It is a far less exacting task intellectually to carve out and polish some specialized slice of an already specialized field of study, such as those mentioned, than it is to follow the inter-disciplinary course, as the pedagogues would call it, that the members of the Wilton Park academic staff must follow.

In addition to meeting all the teaching requirements that have been noted, the Warden of Wilton Park must carry a heavy administrative load. He is the leading architect and organizer of at least ten far-reaching conferences a year and the recruiter of the distinguished leaders in public life to lead discussions at the conferences. 'Here', he has remarked, 'is perhaps the most difficult task of the Warden; to choose topics that are significant for the whole membership and not just the participating country; to balance the opinions put to the conference, and to balance the weight of the speakers, not just the parties or interests they represent; and, finally to recognize

---

1. This was the thrust of his remarks about 'Higher Education in the Free Society' at the inauguration of John Carter Weaver, an 'Old Wiltonian', as Fourteenth President of the University of Missouri on 18 April 1967.

H

issues which will be significant for the future, even if at present few people take an interest in them.'[1]

By one crucial test, the salaries are satisfactory. They keep a notably competent academic staff enthusiastically on the job at Wilton Park and for reasons many of which cannot be calculated in material terms. Of this role Warden Koeppler has said, 'There is great satisfaction in seeing an idea of mine which eventuated in Wilton Park put into practice and seeing it succeed. We do make an important contribution to international understanding, and to having a well informed and thoughtful international public opinion. I am a political animal with a strong urge to play a constructive role in politics. My birth in Germany pretty thoroughly ruled out the possibility of my doing so by having a career in the British Parliament. I like people. Here I have a chance to get to know people with an enormous range of backgrounds, who are generally old enough to have had an interesting range of experience. Our work, about the least repetitive I know of, is breaking new ground all the time. So I am getting paid for doing my political duty in a way I enjoy very much. Perhaps I should be the one to pay for the privilege.'

In more material terms, the Warden has the extraordinarily attractive lodgings as his official quarters which have been previously mentioned. He also manages to maintain his own house, known as the Warden's Keep, in the village of Findon, a very tidy residential community a few miles from Wiston House, where he sleeps and can be by himself when he cares to be. In the domestic arrangements of the Keep there are reflections of the Warden's inventive turn of mind. He has morning coffee there seven days a week but someone to pick up around the place comes only once a week. So the Warden has seven coffee

---

1. 'On working at Wilton Park' in *The Wilton Park Journal*, No. 34, January 1966, p. 11.

makers which are loaded once a week, used one at a time each morning, and washed and refilled once a week.

To satisfy his taste for other than political and social speculation, Warden Koeppler speculates—he prefers the term 'invests'—in a small way in new issues of stocks in British business enterprises. And he speculates in what, it is to be feared, is a large way by testing from time to time— late at night on what he believes to be an open road from London to Wiston House—whether or not his Rover automobile will actually travel the 120 miles an hour it is rated to travel.

### Honours and some complications for the Warden

For Henry Koeppler there has also been the satisfaction of having had his leadership at Wilton Park recognized by honours bestowed by Queen Elizabeth II for notable accomplishment. On 13 June 1957 he (Heinz Koeppler for this purpose) was 'by the Sovereign's command' made an Ordinary Officer of the Civil Division of the Order of the British Empire. And on 1 January 1967 he was named as an Ordinary Commander of the Civil Division of the OBE.

The arraying of his numerous titles in the course of a recent visit to New York City resulted in an amusing incident which, in its way, also provided a reflection of an important aspect of the Warden's character. He was extended guest privileges at one of the city's private residential clubs which entitled him to use its facilities and pay for them just as any regular member of the club would do.

Presumably to impress the staff of the club that Dr Koeppler was no commonplace guest, the secretary of his sponsor, an 'Old Wiltonian', set down the full Koeppler academic and public pedigree in the application for guest privileges. This ran 'H. Koeppler, CBE, MA, DPhil (Oxon), FRHist.S.' Translated this means Commander of the

British Empire, Master of Arts and Doctor of Philosophy of Oxford University and Fellow of the Royal Historical Society.

When, on leaving the club, Henry Koeppler asked for his bill, he received a severe financial shock. The bill struck him as positively astronomical. But, instead of licking his financial wounds quietly and resignedly since he had been a guest, he followed his standard prescription for dealing with the issues that tend to divide us, met the problem presented head-on and sought an explanation of what seemed to him to be an outsize bill.

The explanation turned out to be that the club's book-keeper, new both to the United States and the shorthand of academic titles, thought that H. Koeppler had been the leader of a party of three staying at the club. He had taken the other two in the party to have been D. Phil and F. R. Hist and had calculated the bill for lodging on that basis.

Amid hilarity all round, the Messrs Phil and Hist vanished. Dr Koeppler's bill was adjusted accordingly and he went on his way relieved financially, vastly entertained and, no doubt, a little more confirmed in his conviction that the best way to handle awkward problems, large and small, is to face them frankly.

For the members of the Wilton Park academic staff there are advantages beyond those inherent in their professional roles. Those who have families somehow manage to mobilize the resources to live gracefully in remarkably pleasant surroundings either close by Wiston House or in the town of Steyning. They manage to do this in spite of the fact that Wiston House is located in what has come to be known as Jaguar country. The name is derived from the fact that owning or renting a place has been made expensive by the immigration of so many people, particularly from London, with enough money to drive a Jaguar automobile. For Robert Sturrock, a bachelor who lives at Wiston House during the conferences and has his quarters high in a remote and tranquil corner of the house, there is another advantage. Between conferences he is generally able to get to his beloved Scotland for brief visits and thus to refurbish his delightfully benign detachment in dealing with English political, social and cultural problems. The overseas travel advantages enjoyed by the academic staff members from time to time have already been noted.

### More than a matter of money

Like almost everything else at Wilton Park, the question of whether or not the members of the academic staff make substantial material sacrifices in working there is debatable. If they do, as the composer of this chronicle is inclined to believe they do, they seem to count material rewards that may be somewhat on the slim side as a contribution to doing something to which they are specially devoted. The other members of the staff, paid at rates of pay appropriate to their rank in British government service, make a special contribution to Wilton Park by working with a zest which permeates the enterprise.

Special contributions are also continuously being made to Wilton Park by the VIPs who lead many of its discussions. As has been noted, they receive an honorarium of £15 for an effort for which they could readily command many multiples of this amount in the open market if they elected to do so.

From the entry of £2 425 in the 1971–72 budget for the rental of Wilston House and the upkeep of the grounds, it might seem at first glance that its owner Mr John Goring, is making a tremendous contribution to the operation of Wilton Park. However, the British Department of the Environment maintains the interior structure and regularly makes important capital improvements which in 1970–71 ran to about £5 000.

If the *Wilton Park Journal*, a handsomely printed little semi-annual publication, had been compiled on the pattern of the British Parliamentary *Hansard* or the United States *Congressional Record*, recording everything said at the Wilton Park sessions, it would unquestionably be one of the most revealing records extant of a 25-year development of social, economic and political opinion in the North Atlantic Nations. But the compiling of the record in this way, even if financially feasible, would have put a heavy damper on the spontaneity of the discussions at Wilton Park, conducted as private exchanges of individual and personal opinions.

For a brief period after Wilton Park was converted from a primarily Anglo–German into a European enterprise (in 1957) summaries of the discussions were prepared by groups of participants volunteering to perform this role. The business of having the summaries prepared, edited and reviewed was found to detract from the spontaneity of the discussions. Also the Academic Council felt that it would be difficult, if not impossible, to avoid having them considered official statements in some quarters and that they were not consistent with the promise that the discussions at Wilton Park would be strictly 'off the record'. So the summaries were dropped.

If the leader of the discussions at Wilton Park shows up with a prepared paper of superior quality it generally finds it way into the *Wilton Park Journal*. If the Journal rarely publishes a paper by a British discussion leader, this is not a reflection on the quality of the British performance. Rather it is a reflection of what seems a deep engrained British custom of not preparing papers. The *Journal* is also used on occasion by Warden Koeppler to discuss the Wilton Park programme, and by participants to deal with aspects of the programme they find particularly impressive.

The editorship of the *Journal* is rotated among the members of the academic staff who include notes on interesting and important developments, academic and personal.

In its nature, however, the *Journal* is a fragmentary reference work, so far as recording the history of Wilton Park and appraising its significance is concerned. A well illustrated and descriptive Wilton Park pamphlet, which is revised from time to time and most recently in 1970, provides some help along this line but necessarily not in any great abundance.

The second edition of the history of Wilton Park should have a chapter or two reporting in some detail through interviews with them, on what a broad sampling of those who have enjoyed the generous hospitality of this 'British contribution to the formation of informed international public opinion' have done over the years to make constructive use of their share of the contribution. It would be a fascinating record, and it would also widen the base for generalization about Wilton Park's accomplishments in working toward its objectives during its first quarter of a century.

### Some generalizations about accomplishments

However, the absence of the detailed historical records about Wilton Park's accomplishments as a 'British contribution to the formation of an informed international public opinion' does not foreclose the possibility of some generalizations. One that seems amply justified is that during its operation as an Anglo–German enterprise, Wilton Park was a force of very substantial proportions in healing the inevitably ulcerous post-war relations between Great Britain and Germany and some of Germany's near neighbours in the West. It also seems clear that ideas and knowledge, particularly about the workings of democracy, that were presented and explored at Wilton Park during this period have had a pronounced influence on the development of democracy in post-war Germany. At the twenty-fifth anniversary Wilton Park conference, there was eloquent testimony about the constructive influence of Wilton Park both on Anglo–German relations and the post-war developments of Western Germany.

Another generalization that can be made about Wilton Park in its continuing role as a broadly international institution is that it has given many of its alumni, scattered widely throughout the Western world, an understanding and indeed often an affection for the British way of dealing with political, social, economic and educational problems. In this role of providing what Warden Koeppler has called 'a window on what has been a largely unknown island' Wilton Park is currently making a distinctive contribution to 'the formation of an informed international public opinion'. The absence of any expectation of a *quid pro quo* makes Wilton Park's contributions the more remarkable.

In the nature of the proportions involved—thousands who have been there scattered among hundreds of millions who have not—Wilton Park can hardly be expected to have had a decisive impact in spreading enlightenment about international affairs among the nations from which the participants have come, particularly when such powerful forces of obscurantism are often moving in the opposite direction. But the lack of a triumph in creating international enlightenment does not discount the importance of the contribution of Wilton Park in moving skillfully and persistently to enlarge this area. Some of this success in doing this is attested by the 'Trumpet File', bulging with personal testimonials of Wilton Park's accomplishment in widening the international horizons and deepening the understanding of international affairs of the more than usually influential people in their various lands who have participated in its conferences.

One of the engaging evidences of this influence as a force fostering 'an informed international public opinion' is provided by the numerous efforts of those who have been there to establish institutions patterned on it in their own countries. Among those having such aspirations have been Wilton Park alumni in Germany, France, Switzerland, Italy and the United States.

### Pioneering an American Wilton Park

In the United States in 1972 the American Friends of Wilton Park moved well beyond the stage of simply hoping to have a series of international conferences of the Wilton Park (England) type by: (1) Staging a successful trial run of such a conference, and (2) Adopting plans and getting partial financial support for two more.

At Wingspread, the home of the Johnson Foundation at Racine, Wisconsin, a two-day meeting in July 1972 was jointly devoted to a Wilton Park type conference on the changing nature of Atlantic relations and discussing the need of a Wilton Park in America and, given the need, what might be done about it. The trial run of a Wilton Park type conference was organized and led by Dean Peter F. Krogh of the School of Foreign Service of Georgetown University, Washington, DC. In dealing with the question of the need of a Wilton Park in America and, granted the need, how to get it successfully established, the meeting had the benefit of a year's work done by a planning committee, headed by Robert Rankin, Vice President of the Danforth Foundation of St Louis, Missouri.[1]

The conclusion about the need of an American Wilton Park, ratified by the American Friends of Wilton Park at their annual meeting the day after the two-day conference and planning session, was that the need is very real. It was recognized that there is an abundance of conferences,

---

1. Other members of the planning committee were Dean Krogh, Congressman Charles Mosher, Mr Zygmunt Nagorski, Director of Programs for the Council on Foreign Relations and President of the American Friends of Wilton Park, Dr William Olson, Director of the Rockefeller Foundation at the Villa Serbelloni at Bellagio, Italy, the first President of the American Friends of Wilton Park, and Dr Paul Schratz, Director, Office of International Studies, University of Missouri, USA.

I

domestic and international, in the United States but a serious paucity, if not a total lack, of international conferences with the distinctive features of those conducted at the British Wilton Park which have been underlined in this chronicle.

In developing a Wilton Park in the United States it was agreed that the initial focus should be on Atlantic relations, with the participants drawn from the United States, Canada and Western Europe. Programmes devoted to a broader range of international relations would come later. Among the reasons for initial concentration on Atlantic relations was the judgement of those at the Wingspread meetings that 'the potential for Europe and America to drift apart is greater today than it has been for most of the post-war period' and the further judgement that there is need for much more mutual trans-Atlantic understanding 'during a period of transition in American foreign policy' than there is at present.

The effort to establish an American Wilton Park was given a big lift by The Johnson Foundation at the annual meeting of the American Friends. Leslie Paffrath, the President of the Foundation, invited them to conduct two five-day international Wilton Park type conferences during the following eighteen months at the Foundation's Wingspread conference centre and offered to help finance them, as it had helped to finance the trial run conference and planning meetings prior to the annual meeting. The Johnson Foundation provided the conference facilities of Wingspread, including meals and lodging for the participants, and assistance to the Planning Committee.[1] The Crown Zellerbach Foundation, with headquarters in San Francisco, helped to defray the transportation

1. The Johnson Foundation has (among many other philanthropic and educational activities) for a decade convened meetings at Wingspread to advance American–West European mutual understanding. Thus support of an American Wilton Park fits neatly into the programme of the Foundation.

expenses of participants in these meetings who could not get there otherwise.

Over the eighteen months, during which The Johnson Foundation undertook to give major support to two Wilton Park type international conferences at Wingspread, it was agreed that strenuous efforts would be made to raise money from both public and private sources to get a full-fledged American Wilton Park established. Robert Rankin, re-christened the Chairman of the Steering Committee rather than the Planning Committee, was put in charge of this operation. Warden Koeppler of the parent or perhaps better cousin British Wilton Park was at the sessions where the American Wilton Park was launched, and wished Godspeed to the enterprise. It had the specially influential support of Dr John C. Weaver, President of the University of Wisconsin, an 'Old Wiltonian' and a Trustee of The Johnson Foundation.

The development of a Wilton Park in the United States is not to be at the expense of efforts by the American Friends of Wilton Park to get Americans to the conferences at Wilton Park, England. This, it was resolved at the Wingspread meeting, remains the top priority purpose of the American Friends. The by-laws of the organization give first priority to 'assuring participation by qualified persons in the Wilton Park conferences' in England.

It is a most impressive tribute to the British Wilton Park that there should have been so many impulses to create replicas of it in other parts of the Western World, one of which got well off the ground at Wingspread. And, as was clearly recognized at Wingspread, the replicas do not need to be anything like exact copies in order to embody many and perhaps even most of Wilton Park's distinctive and constructive features, such as its particularly stimulating discussions techniques, its determined rejection of a narrowly specialized approach to international problems and its maintenance of a time span for its conferences

long enough and so paced and arranged as to lubricate a
free but friendly exchange of ideas and opinions about
what may be very thorny subjects.

## A man for all nations

There is no reason to expect, however, that the Wilton
Park design, as a total entity, would be an adaptable
transplant to other countries. In some of them there would
be the problem of reconciling preponderant financial
support by the government and academic freedom of the
sort prevailing at Wilton Park. In many and indeed probably
in most countries the political leaders could not be counted
upon to take the tough questioning on sensitive issues
by people from many other countries that British political
leaders at Wilton Park take gracefully in their stride.
The blend of the Elizabethan and the very modern in the
Wiston House setting, and the blend of warm hospitality
and authoritative call to hard work would be difficult to
duplicate. And, probably pre-eminently, there would be
the surely refractory problem of providing the inspiring
type of leadership that Wilton Park has had.

'Isn't it odd to have a man of German origin running
such a peculiarly British institution as Wilton Park?'
was the musing of a member of the Wilton Park Academic
Council. Perhaps the answer was provided by a visitor to
Wilton Park in its very early days at Beaconsfield, who
remarked that it was being 'run by a man who has become
completely English without ceasing to be a German'.[1]
In the subsequent development of Wilton Park on a
broadly international base, someone observing how much
at home the Warden seems to feel when visiting and
teaching in the United States might remark, 'Isn't it
odd to have Wilton Park run by a man who has become
so completely American without ceasing to be British

1. 'Weekend at Wilton Park' by Patrick Gordon Walker, MP, published
   in *The Changing Nation*, Contact Book, 1 January 1948.

and German?' His joint German and British background is reflected in the fact that he speaks Oxford English with a slight German accent or, as a member of the academic staff has put it, 'with the vowels of Oxford fighting the consonants of Berlin'. The Warden says he could have shed the accent while a student at Oxford if his fellow students had not found it enjoyable and encouraged him to keep it.

All of this is not by any means to say that the Warden is a sort of litmus-like character, reflecting the attributes of peoples and nations as he moves among them physically. On the contrary, he is a man of very strong basic political convictions, one of which—his complete commitment to a democratic way of life—he demonstrated by leaving his homeland and becoming a British citizen when Hitler gained ascendancy in Germany. Another of his profound political convictions is that the strength of the Atlantic Community is the keystone to the political well being of the Western World and that its cohesiveness is to be cherished accordingly. Some of those who have followed the discussions at Wilton Park have jokingly remarked that the session may be labelled as concentrating on problems of the developing countries or international aspects of space exploration but that, before the end, there is sure to be some concentration on the crucial importance of maintaining a strong Atlantic Community.

While his political convictions go deep, so does the Warden's capacity to think and feel across international boundaries. He also has the capacity to think and feel across partisan political lines in British politics. 'I am afraid I wouldn't make a very good party whip', he has remarked. 'I see what seem to me strengths and weaknesses in the positions of all of our major political parties, Conservative, Labour and Liberal alike. This is not conducive to taking a comfortable partisan position on most important political issues in Britain.' However, it does seem to be conducive to phenomenal success in pursuading leaders of all of these parties to lead discussions at Wilton Park. Indeed a member of his Academic Council has remarked, 'The Warden is successful to a rare degree in getting British leaders to come and work hard at Wilton Park and making them friends of Wilton Park after they get here'. This success has also extended in notable degree to leaders in other countries of Western Europe.

This same member of the Academic Council also said of Wilton Park, 'Of course, it is the Warden's show'. The Warden would deny this. In support of his denial he would cite the fact that, faced with the decision of the Foreign Office in 1956 to close it, Wilton Park would not even exist today if he had not had the help of a broad cross section of political leadership, particularly in Britain. He would surely also make the contention that, without his talented staff, Wilton Park would be but a pale shadow of what it is. However, there is enough truth in the characterization of Wilton Park as the Warden's 'show' to raise questions about how and where it goes when the Warden goes. Happily, the Warden's surging vigour and vitality do not suggest that the questions are for the near future. Indeed, 'without putting the Wilton Park programme at risk', to use the British Foreign Office's expression, he has recently added to his labours the leadership of a European Discussion Centre at Wiston House where representatives of the countries in the enlarged European Economic Community will confer—perhaps at ten week-end or five one-week meetings a year—about Community problems and possibilities.

But questions about the future of Wilton Park without the Warden are still there. Commenting obliquely on the view that it is Warden Koeppler's 'show' and would cease to be its essential self without him, one of the members of the Wilton Park community has remarked, 'It's true, isn't it, that most great restaurants have a life of twenty-five or thirty years, which is about the working life of a great chef. Can we expect a longer life for Wilton Park?' While the Warden would probably not be offended by the equating of his work at Wilton Park with that of a great chef, his answer would be and the answer should be, 'Yes, we can and certainly should expect and see to it that Wilton Park has a life extending far beyond the career there of any individual or group of individuals'.

Wilton Park is the embodiment of ideas, methods, and an environment which in combination make for a great institution whose life tenure should be viewed in that light.

The programme of the

# 133rd Wilton Park Conference[1]

## 20 June to 3 July 1971

*To commemorate the Twenty-fifth Anniversary of the foundation of Wilton Park*

Wilton Park is a British contribution to the formation of an informed international public opinion. To promote greater cooperation in Europe and the West in general, it offers those influencing opinion in their own countries an opportunity of exchanging views on political, economic and social questions of common interest.

Every Wilton Park Conference deals with a broad range of these problems.

Within this framework some sessions of each conference are devoted to a specific aspect which, however, does not dominate the conference, since Wilton Park avoids narrow specialization.

The specific aspect of this Conference will be:

TWENTY-FIVE YEARS OF CHANGE: IN GREAT BRITAIN AND IN INTERNATIONAL RELATIONS

1. The programme of this conference was more tightly packed with scheduled meetings than the usual Wilton Park conference. Reason: the opportunity to meet, hear from and talk with a Jubilee array of discussion leaders and hosts.

Sunday 20 June

  Members arrive at Wilton Park

**After
dinner**    The WARDEN At Home


Monday 21 June

**Morning**    WILTON PARK: AN APOLOGIA
The discussion will be opened by the WARDEN

THE SCOPE OF THE CONFERENCE
The discussion will be opened by the WARDEN

**Afternoon**    INAUGURAL SESSION
The discussion will be opened by
The Rt. Hon. Edward HEATH, MBE, MP
Prime Minister

A RECEPTION
to be followed by a DINNER in honour of the
PRIME MINISTER

**Evening**    DISCUSSION GROUPS
in English:    *Mr O. G. Hayward*
in French:    *Mr H. B. Shepherd*
        *Mr R. S. Sturrock*
in German:    *Mr K. W. Lauermann*
It is suggested that each of the above and the subsequent
discussion group sessions should be opened by a
Member of the Conference


Tuesday 22 June

The following speakers from
    FRANCE
    GERMANY and
    SPAIN
will open discussions during the course of the day:—

Monsieur Léo HAMON
Sécretaire d'État auprès du Premier Ministre; porte-
    parole du Gouvernement
EUROPE IN THE SEVENTIES

Herr Helmut H. W. Schmidt, M. d. B.
Minister of Defence of the Federal Republic of Germany
EUROPEAN PARTNERSHIP AND ATLANTIC ALLIANCE

General Manuel DIEZ-ALEGRIA
Chief of the Spanish Defence Staff
EUROPEAN SECURITY PROBLEMS IN THE TWENTY FIVE YEARS SINCE WORLD WAR II

Discussion Groups will also take place

### Wednesday 23 June

**Morning**     Discussion groups
        in English:    *Mr K. W. Lauermann*
                *Mr R. S. Sturrock*
        in French:    *Mr H. B. Shepherd*
        in German:    *Mr O. G. Hayward*

THE PROBLEMS IN INTERNATIONAL AFFAIRS DURING THE NEXT TWENTY-FIVE YEARS: A LIBERAL POINT OF VIEW
The discussion will be opened by
The Rt Hon. Jeremy THORPE, MP.
Liberal Member of Parliament for North Devon; Leader of the Liberal Party

**Afternoon**    THE EVOLUTION AND THE FUTURE OF NATO
The discussion will be opened by
Sir Frank ROBERTS, GCMG, GCVO
Advisory Director of Unilever and Adviser on International Affairs to Lloyds; President, The British Atlantic Committee; formerly United Kingdom Permanent Representative on the North Atlantic Council and Ambassador to the USSR and the Federal Republic of Germany

**Evening**     THE EVOLUTION OF STRATEGY AND THE POWER BALANCE

The discussion will be opened by
Brigadier W. F. K. THOMPSON, OBE
Defence Correspondent, 'The Daily Telegraph'

Thursday 24 June

Extra-mural day    London

Meetings and visits will be arranged in accordance with Members' wishes; interpretation in French and German will be provided

A LUNCHEON
for the Members of the Conference has been arranged in the
HOUSE OF COMMONS
which will be preceded by a Tour of the
PALACE OF WESTMINSTER
Mr Douglas Dodds-Parker, MP will preside over the luncheon

During the late afternoon, a
RECEPTION
will be given at LANCASTER HOUSE by
HER MAJESTY'S GOVERNMENT
in honour of the Members of the Conference
The Most Hon. THE MARQUESS and
MARCHIONESS OF LOTHIAN will receive the guests

Friday 25 June

**Morning**    Discussion groups
in preparation for the International Round Table Session
in English:    *Mr R. S. Sturrock*
in French:    *Mr O. G. Hayward*
                 *Mr H. B. Shepherd*
in German:    *Mr K. W. Lauermann*

TWENTY-FIVE YEARS OF CHANGE IN INTER-NATIONAL RELATIONS:
THE POINT OF VIEW OF A YUGOSLAV
The discussion will be opened by
Dr Leo MATES
Director, The Institute of International Politics and Economy, Belgrade; formerly Permanent Yugoslav Representative at the United Nations and Ambassador to the United States

**Afternoon**     TWENTY-FIVE YEARS OF THE COMMON-
WEALTH
The discussion will be opened by
Professor Max BELOFF
Gladstone Professor of Government and Public
Administration, University of Oxford; Fellow of
All Souls; Author of a number of works on political,
constitutional, and historical subjects, including
'Imperial Sunset'; Member of the Wilton Park
Academic Council

**Evening**     THE DEVELOPMENT OF NATIONALISM SINCE
1945
The discussion will be opened by
Professor Sir Robert BIRLEY, KCMG
Head of the Department of Social Science and
Humanities, City University, London; Chairman
of the Wilton Park Academic Council

**Saturday 26 June**

**Morning**     Discussion groups
in English:   *Mr O. G. Hayward*
in French:    *Mr H. B. Shepherd*
*Mr R. S. Sturrock*
in German:   *Mr K. W. Lauermann*

INDUSTRIAL RELATIONS
The discussion will be opened by
Mr Victor FEATHER, CBE
General Secretary, The Trades Union Congress

**Afternoon**     THE HUMAN FACTOR OF THE CANADIAN
NORTH
The discussion will be opened by
Dr A. W. R. CARROTHERS, President and Vice-
Chancellor, University of Calgary, Alberta, Canada

**Evening**     CONGRESSIONAL INFLUENCE UPON AMERI-
CAN FOREIGN POLICY
The discussion will be opened by
Dr William OLSON
Vice-President, The Rockefeller Foundation; Director
of the Villa Serbelloni, Bellagio; Chairman of the
Board of the American Friends of Wilton Park

Sunday 27 and Monday 28 June

On Sunday

A coach journey has been arranged to
OXFORD via
WINCHESTER,
SALISBURY and
STONEHENGE
Sunday night will be spent in Oxford

On Monday

A tour of some of the Colleges will take place in the
morning,
followed by a
CELEBRATION LUNCHEON
in the HALL OF MAGDALEN COLLEGE
(by kind permission of the President and Fellows of the
College),
at which Senior Members of the University and their
wives will be present
Dr James GRIFFITHS, OBE, President of Magdalen
College and Sir William HAYTER, KCMG, Vice-
Chairman of the Wilton Park Academic Council
and Warden of New College will speak during the
Luncheon

Return to Wiston House in time for dinner

Tuesday 29 June

**Morning**   GREAT BRITAIN AND THE WORLD, 1945–1971:
A LABOUR POINT OF VIEW
The discussion will be opened by
The Rt. Hon. Roy JENKINS, MP

Labour Member of Parliament for the Stechford
Division of Birmingham; Deputy Leader of the
Labour Party; formerly Chancellor of the Exchequer

**Afternoon**   CHANGES IN THE CULTURAL SCENE
The discussion will be opened by
The Rt. Rev. THE BISHOP OF CHICHESTER
Member of the Wilton Park Academic Council

**Evening**        Discussion groups
                in English:  *Mr K W Lauermann*
                in French:   *Mr H. B. Shepherd*
                             *Mr R. S. Sturrock*
                in German:   *Mr O. G. Hayward*

Wednesday 30 June

**Morning**       Discussion groups
                in English:  *Mr H. B. Shepherd*
                in French:   *Mr O. G. Hayward*
                             *Mr R. S. Sturrock*
                in German:   *Mr K. W. Lauermann*

                TWENTY-FIVE YEARS OF CHANGE IN THE
                CIVIL SERVICE
                The discussion will be opened by
                Sir William ARMSTRONG, GCB, MVO
                Head of the Home Civil Service and Permanent
                Secretary to the Civil Service Department

**Afternoon**     TWENTY-FIVE YEARS OF BRITISH POLICY
                The discussion will be opened by
                The Rt. Hon. Kenneth YOUNGER
                Director, The Royal Institute of International Affairs;
                Member of the Wilton Park Academic Council

**Evening**       THE EVOLUTION OF PARLIAMENT
                The discussion will be opened by
                Professor Esmond WRIGHT
                Director Designate, The Institute of United States
                Studies and Professor of American History, Univer-
                sity of London; formerly Conservative Member of
                Parliament for the Pollock Division of Glasgow

Thursday 1 July

**Morning**       INTERNATIONAL ROUND TABLE
                Some Members of the Conference will be invited to
                open a Plenary Discussion
                This will be followed by a continuation of the Dis-
                cussion or by Discussion groups

Afternoon    TWENTY-FIVE YEARS OF CHANGE:
             A DANISH POINT OF VIEW
             The discussion will be opened by
             Mr Poul HARTLING
             Danish Minister of Foreign Affairs

Evening      THE MEDIA AND PUBLIC OPINION
             The discussion will be opened by
             The Rt. Hon. R. H. S. CROSSMAN, OBE, MP
             Editor, 'The New Statesman'; Labour Member of
             Parliament for Coventry East; formerly Secretary
             of State for Social Services

Friday 2 July

Morning      Discussion groups
             in English:    Mr K. W. Lauermann
                            Mr R. S. Sturrock
             in French:     Mr H. B. Shepherd
             in German:     Mr O. G. Hayward

             VITAL ISSUES IN INTERNATIONAL RELATIONS
             SINCE THE WAR:
             A DUTCH POINT OF VIEW
             The discussion will be opened by
             Dr J. M. A. H. LUNS, GCMG
             Netherlands Minister of Foreign Affairs

Late
Afternoon    FINAL SESSION OF THE CONFERENCE
             The discussion will be opened by
             Sir Denis GREENHILL, KCMG, OBE
             Permanent Under-Secretary of State, Foreign and
             Commonwealth Office; Head of Her Majesty's
             Diplomatic Service

Evening      A RECEPTION in honour of Sir Denis GREENHILL
             to be followed by
             FAREWELL DINNER

Saturday 3 July

             Free day in London and departure for home